Nevins, J.B.

A Narrative of two Voyages to Hudson's Bay

Inktank publishing

Nevins, J.B.

A Narrative of two Voyages to Hudson's Bay

Inktank publishing, 2018

www.inktank-publishing.com

ISBN/EAN: 9783747768747

All rights reserved

This is a reprint of a historical out of copyright text that has been re-manufactured for better reading and printing by our unique software. Inktank publishing retains all rights of this specific copy which is marked with an invisible watermark.

A

NARRATIVE OF TWO VOYAGES

TO

HUDSON'S BAY,

WITH

TRADITIONS OF THE NORTH AMERICAN INDIANS.

By J. B. NEVINS, M.D. Lond.

PUBLISHED UNDER THE DIRECTION OF
THE COMMITTEE OF GENERAL LITERATURE AND EDUCATION,
APPOINTED BY THE SOCIETY FOR PROMOTING
CHRISTIAN KNOWLEDGE.

LONDON:
PRINTED FOR THE
SOCIETY FOR PROMOTING CHRISTIAN KNOWLEDGE;
SOLD AT THE DEPOSITORY,
GREAT QUEEN STREET, LINCOLN'S INN FIELDS;
AND 4, ROYAL EXCHANGE.
1847.

PREFACE.

In the following Work it must be noticed, that the descriptions of the Indians and Esquimaux of the Hudson's Bay Territory, only apply to the tribes met with near the borders of Hudson's Bay, which are principally the Chippewa and Cree Indians. This remark is necessary, because the account here given differs in some respects from what has been published concerning the tribes inhabiting the plains and the interior of the country. The general term Indian, embraces many nations, which differ exceedingly in size, strength, appearance, and habits: whenever the

Author has mentioned anything concerning them, without giving an authority for it, the circumstances have fallen under his own observation; and he has the most perfect reliance upon the veracity of the Indian chief, from whom he received the traditions related in the following pages.

Liverpool, 1847.

A NARRATIVE,

&c.

We sailed from London on the 4th of June 1842, in the "good ship Prince Rupert, bound,"—according to the reverential phrase, introduced when voyages were even more rare and dangerous than at present, and still retained in ships' papers,—"by the Grace of God, to York Factory, Hudson's Bay."

A summer voyage to this place is not quite so easy or pleasant as an excursion up the Rhine, or down the Danube. And not only must the crew be provided with an extra supply of winter clothing to guard against the cold, but the ship must also be protected against the violent blows she receives from the large masses of ice floating, even in summer, throughout the northern seas. This is done by making her sides double where they are most exposed, and by putting very thick, strong caseings of wood, called ice-chocks, in front of her bows, which add to her strength, though, it must be confessed, they diminish her beauty.

We sailed first to Stromness, in the Orkney Islands, where we remained nearly a fortnight to take some men on board, several of whom go from Orkney every year as labourers in the service of

B

the Hudson's Bay Company; and though the wages are very low, and they have to endure great hardships and privations, there is so much spirit of enterprize amongst the inhabitants of these islands, that there is little difficulty in obtaining a sufficient number. The custom was so general a few years since, that a person was scarcely considered a man, until he had been to the "nor'-west," and he would stand but an indifferent chance of a favourable reception, should he make proposals of marriage before having given this proof of his manhood; but this feeling is now less strong than it was, and many of the labourers are married before going out.

After leaving Stromness, we sailed direct for Hudson's Straits, and had the usual amount of comforts and annoyances experienced in a sea voyage; but met with nothing of particular interest after passing Rona, until we approached the entrance of the Straits. That island appears at a little distance to be nothing but a bleak and desolate rock, though a few fishermen live upon one part of it. There is so little intercourse between it and other places, that it is said George the Third was prayed for, three months after his death, the news not having reached the island sooner.

The weather was generally pretty fine, but was very thick and disagreeable off the south of Greenland. This region goes amongst sailors by the name of the "Stormy Forties;" and it is curious that whatever the weather may have been in other places, it is generally rough or foggy between 40° and 50° west longitude. If it had been clear, we might from the mast-head have seen Staten Hook, the southern portion of Greenland, which is very lofty; but as it was, we saw nothing. For several days it continued so thick as to prevent our taking any observation of the sun, and thereby ascertaining our exact position. It cleared up one afternoon, and we saw land distinctly, which we supposed to be Hatton's Headland, the south cape of Resolution Island, at the mouth of Hudson's Straits, and it was so entered in the log-book.

The weather again became thick, and the wind so contrary, that we were tossing about for four days, unable to enter the Straits, and waiting for it to clear. When this happened we found we had been quite mistaken. There is always a strong current down the south side of Hudson's Straits, which in some places runs as fast as seven or eight knots an hour. This had caught us, and carried us even below Cape Chidlegh, on the north of Labrador, the point of land we had observed. It must be very lofty, for at the time we saw it, we were not less than sixty or seventy miles distant.

We were sailing smoothly along six days before entering the Strait, when the man on the look out called out "Ice a-head!" and we soon saw some small pieces floating slowly towards us. Later on in the afternoon, we came into the midst of a small field of ice, which we soon left behind. To those who had not seen any before, it appeared a good deal; and we congratulated each other upon our good fortune in seeing what so few people have the opportunity of doing, viz., large fields of ice in the middle of July. There is really more beauty in these small pieces, than in the larger masses, or even in the icebergs themselves. By small pieces must be understood masses varying from three or four feet square, and the same depth, to the size of a common two-storied house. When these are collected so as to appear at a little distance like a single sheet of ice, they are called fields; and when a mass is one or two hundred feet long, and two or three hundred feet deep, then it is called an iceberg.

There is a remarkable beauty about many of the smaller pieces, both in the forms which they present, and in their colours. The ice is seldom white, except in some of the largest bergs, but has generally many exquisite shades, from the faintest trace to a deep sky-blue. These shades do not depend upon the reflected colour of the water, for they are equally visible in the middle of a large mass which is not within forty or fifty feet of it; nor are they owing to the colour of the sky, for they are as visible on a cloudy as on a fine day, and are generally the deepest in the interior of he ice. A piece often looks snow-white externally, but on scraping off the loose, external covering, the ice underneath is hard and blue, and sometimes even shines through the white exterior.

There is scarcely any form which the ice does not at times assume. From the washing by the waves it is broken away in different parts, and the under portion is melted, leaving elegant overhanging pieces, like the expanded wings of some beautiful swan. You may often fancy that you see these birds with their graceful necks and white wings floating quietly past the ship, whilst at other times the ice resembles a stag with its branching horns, or an old ruined castle, or some strange and beautiful animal. The pieces are almost constantly rising and falling in the water, and all around is heard the dashing of the little waves, as they pour through the many holes and arches which are gradually washed away, whilst the white foam is tossed in every direction.

It is very difficult to form a correct estimate of the depth of the ice under water, which has been variously stated by Franklin, Parry, Ross, and others; some saying that for every foot above water, there are ten feet below, whilst others think there are but four. Perhaps both are right; the fact is, that the weight of two pieces of ice of the same size often differs considerably. The variety in the shape of the icebergs makes an immense difference in this respect, for some rise very high, but consist only of one or two slender peaks, whilst others are solid and square, and have much more depth out of sight.

There is also another circumstance, which I think has caused some mistakes. It is not very unusual to see an iceberg quite stationary, whilst the small pieces of ice are floating rapidly past it; and in such cases the sea having been sounded and found to be from eighty to two hundred fathoms, that is, from four hundred and eighty to twelve hundred feet deep, it has been supposed that the iceberg must have been resting on the bottom, from its being immoveable. But there are often two currents at different depths, running in opposite directions at the same time,

B 3

which is discovered in the following manner:—If a heavy piece of lead is tied to a line and thrown overboard it will sink. We will suppose that the current at the surface of the water is running from west to east, which is usually more or less the case in Hudson's Strait; when the lead has been allowed to descend sixty or eighty fathoms, it comes into a current running from east to west. If we tie a buoy to the end of the line, it will float and keep the lead from sinking. Now the under current would carry the lead towards the west; but it cannot move in this direction, because the upper current would carry the buoy towards the east, and thus they both remain stationary. The small pieces of ice which are not so deep as to feel the under current, would now float past the buoy; and if this were an iceberg, we should think that it must be at the bottom of the sea, because it did not move.

Every one would probably be disappointed by the first sight of an iceberg. At a considerable distance may be seen a small white mass, which perhaps does not look larger than the palm of the hand; and the sailors, being accustomed to judge of the size of objects at a distance, will say—"There is a large iceberg. It is as high as the top of our masts. That berg is not less than six hundred feet high." The spectator might begin to think—"St. Paul's is about four hundred feet high, so that is half as high again." He would not perhaps remember, that four or five hundred feet of its height were below the water, and that he was too far off to see its real size; thus he would be disappointed, and think that it looked very small. It is only after having seen a good many, and perhaps played at foot-ball upon them, that he begins to entertain a proper respect for them. We sailed past one which was so high, that when I went about eighty feet up the mast, I could scarcely see over it. It was solid in appearance, so that I have no doubt it was between five and six hundred feet below the water. Another morning we sailed close along the side of an iceberg which was about forty feet above the water; but this was nearly three miles long, and above half a mile broad. We could see four white bears upon it, with the telescope, and the water on the other side. We knew that it was not an island, because there is none in that part of the Strait. A night or two after this we sailed past another, which, however, I did not see. The mate told me that we were about an hour in sailing past it, and we were going nearly seven knots an hour.

When they are of such extent as these, they look just like islands covered with snow; and it is only by seeing the side or end that you can tell it is ice. There is a very large iceberg in Davis' Strait, which has been for many years in the same place, and alters so little that ships steer by it. It is exceedingly dangerous to be very near one in the autumn; for, when they have had the heat and washing of the summer seas, they become worn away, and at length break into two or more pieces, which roll over time after time, until at length they are settled. If the iceberg has been deep, its bottom striking the bottom or side of the ship as it rolled over, would be likely to damage it materially, even if it did not burst it in or upset it. I never saw a large iceberg fall in two, but I have seen many small ones; and several large ones which were so far split, that the first heavy wave must have broken them in pieces. One of the most surprising things about them is their hardness. We were sailing slowly past a very large one, which came down to the water's edge, almost like a wall, and from which we were distant about two hundred yards. The captain desired that one of the guns should be loaded with a ball weighing twelve pounds, and when fired the ball struck it fairly, made a little dent in it, and fell off into the water. It seems most probable that these large icebergs are many years in forming, and that they come down the straits and bays which open into Hudson's Strait. All the islands and coasts are rocky and very steep, and many of them are several hundred feet high. In winter, when the sea freezes under them, the iceberg begins to form; afterwards, a heavy fall of snow makes it somewhat higher; in summer, some of this snow melts, but does not run off the top; at least, the whole of it does not, for there is generally a good deal of fresh water upon them. The snow upon the land melts much sooner than that upon the ice, and the water drops or runs off the overhanging edges of the rocks upon the ice below; the nights being cold, it freezes again. The next winter comes another fall of snow, and in the spring more water; which, trickling down, freezes, and makes all solid. So it goes on, until the body of ice becomes so large and heavy, that some time, when the sea perhaps is rough, it breaks off from the rocks, and is carried by the current downwards into Hudson's Strait. It seems impossible that they could become so large in a single year; and, besides this, we always see several in the inlets along the north coast of the Strait in coming home in autumn; now they cannot have formed during the summer, and it is not likely that they would be broken up after that time, as winter is then approaching.

We expected to see some of the Esquimaux in sailing up the Strait, as they generally come from some of the islands on the north coast. For several days before we saw them, we were busy making preparation for what the sailors call "the Huskie* trade," and speculating upon what we were likely to get from them.

The ships keep pretty close to the north coast in sailing up the Strait, because it is much more free from ice than the south side. The current generally runs from west to east and somewhat towards the south, so that the ice is carried towards that shore, and leaves the north clear. The land looks most dismal and bleak in sailing past. It is often covered with snow, and even where this has disappeared, it looks only like barren, dark rocks. No trees, no grass, not even any green moss can be seen growing upon it. Sometimes it is possible to observe something through the telescope which looks like heather, and there must be some sort of coarse grass, which grows perhaps at

* I imagine that this term is thus derived: Esquimaux is a long word for sailors to use, so it has been shortened into Eskies, which has been easily changed into Heskies; and some northcountryman has added strength to the sound, and converted it into Huskies.

a distance from the shore, for some of the Esquimaux wore little hats without brims made of this material. There is one part which is called Terra Nieva, because it has never been seen without snow upon it.

We passed Grass or Green Island at such a distance, that we could only just see it from the mast-head ; but we saw Saddleback distinctly, which is one of the group of islands called Middle Savage. It is usual to see some Esquimaux here, so as we sailed past we fired several guns, to give them notice of our arrival ; but none came. On Saturday afternoon, July the 30th, we were opposite Upper Savage Islands, and we knew that if we did not see them here, we should probably miss them altogether. As the wind was light, and we were not doing much good, we shortened sail, and fired several guns, and kept sailing backwards and forwards, towards and from the island, all the afternoon. We began almost to despair of seeing them, for none were in sight at tea-time. However, about 7 P. M. we saw, on looking through the telescope towards the shore, a little black speck in the water, which we had not noticed before, and sometimes there was a small bright spot for a moment near it. All was now excitement, and every one was anxious to get the glass. In a short time the black spot seemed larger, and one or two others were in sight. Long before we could see them distinctly, so as to distinguish the man from the canoe, we heard their cry of Chimoo ! Chimoo ! which is their interjection of delight. Their canoes are made of laths of wood tied together with sinew, so as to give the shape they want;

they are sharp at each end, and nearly flat-bottomed, so that they will float in very little water. Over this frame they stretch seal-skins very tightly which have had the hair scraped off, and are then sewn together with sinews. The skins come over the top, as well as the sides and ends; and they leave a hole in the middle, just large enough for a man to sit down in, so that when he is seated, if the waves were to wash over it, they would not get inside. When completed they are light enough to be easily carried, if they should come to a field of ice whilst out fishing or hunting. They appear very unsafe, and as though they would easily roll over, and I believe that they do not go out in them if the sea is rough, for they never come to the ship unless it is smooth and calm. They have only a single paddle, which they hold by the middle, and dipping the ends alternately over the opposite sides of the canoe, they make them move very quickly. The paddles are about ten feet long, and round in the middle, but a little broader at the end, and flat. Some of them are very nicely ornamented with ivory, which they get from the walruses or sea-horses. This they make into thin layers, which they put upon the edges and tips of their paddles, which not only makes them look better, but causes them to last much longer than wood alone would do.

In a short time, there were about thirty canoes round the ship, and it was very amusing to see the way in which the trade was carried on. They had brought a considerable quantity of ivory and whalebone, and this was the most valuable part of the trade; but what interested me most were some little models of their canoes, which were lying upon the top of those they were in, and their spears which they use in hunting. The trade is carried on in a very simple way. Iron is what they particularly wish for, and a good saw is what they most value. I suppose they use it for cutting up the ivory. Next to this they like a hatchet, and then a knife; and, what we should think very strange, they will take a piece of an old iron hoop almost as readily as anything. When we left England I did not know that we should see any of them, so that I had not provided anything for trading with—but I soon found that a few needles would go a long way; and half a paper of strong darning needles, and a paper of common tailor's needles, which I had bought in Stromness, were quite sufficient to set me up.

The captain, who was the chief trader, and bought all the ivory and whalebone, and the few furs and skins which they had with them, took a saw in his hand, and rattled it against the side of the ship. In a minute the men in the nearest canoes caught up the walrus tusks, which they had, and held them up in exchange. Seeing they had plenty of ivory, perhaps more was asked for the saw than it was worth. The tusks were tied together, and sometimes there were four or five, sometimes eight or ten, in the bundle, which would weigh several pounds. The greatest number which was held up at first was eight; the captain shook his head, and continued rattling the saw. There was presently a rummage inside the canoe; two or three

Google

more were found; and these were accepted as sufficient. Then another saw was held up, or a hatchet. If they had been some time without a saw, they began crying out, "Cuttee-swaback, Cuttee-swaback;" and imitating the motion by sawing most industriously with their arms in the air. Some of them had no ivory; but whalebone answered as well, provided there was plenty of it.

After looking on for some time, I began to think of doing a little business for myself, so running down into my berth I got my paper of needles and came again upon deck. I saw what seemed a pretty little model of a canoe, and calling Chimoo, because I did not know any other word, I pointed to what I wanted, and held up four needles. Immediately the man pushed his canoe between the others, and the purchase was soon finished. When a bargain is concluded, each party holds up his hands, and cries out "Chimoo! Chimoo!" to show that he is pleased with what he has got. Whatever is given to the Esquimaux he licks on both sides, holds up for admiration, and then puts out of the way in his canoe. Whether it is a saw, a hatchet, a razor, or a rusty piece of hoop, it undergoes this process, and the purchaser perhaps thinks he can judge of its quality by this means. The needles were put into their mouths, and kept there, until they had time to put them away in safety. When I had received my purchase upon deck, it did not look quite so well as it did at a distance, so I bought two or three more, in hopes of getting a nice one at last. I paid the same price for each, and was very well satisfied, until I found that some of the sailors had only given two needles for theirs, when I began to think I had been sadly cheated.

I bought two of their spears, which are very pretty, and ingeniously made, on the same terms. No trees grow upon these islands, so they can only get drift-wood, which is carried by the waves from other places. They take a straight piece of this, about four feet long, and bore a hole through one end of it. Then they take a straight piece of ivory, which they sharpen at one end, and through the other end bore another hole. They can then tie this to the wooden shaft with a piece of sinew, or a thong made of seal-skin. But as they may perhaps miss what they have thrown it at with the point, they make an addition to it in this way. They take three curved pieces of ivory, about nine inches long, which they grind into a sharp point at one end. Then they tie these at equal distances round the shaft of the spear about its middle; so that one end of each piece is made fast close to the shaft, whilst the other, which is the sharp end, sticks out about four or five inches from it. It looks when finished rather like the pictures of Neptune's trident, or still more like what an arrow would be, if one end of each of the three feathers, which are tied round it to make it fly steadily, were left loose, and sticking out from the shaft. In this way, if they miss the bird or seal at which they have shot with the point of the spear, they will most likely hit it with one of these projecting points in the middle. One of the spears which I bought was still bloody from a bird which the man had shot upon the water as he was coming to the ship, and some of its feathers were sticking in it. The bird was lying upon the top of his canoe. It is to make spear points that they wish so much for iron hoop, which they break into short pieces, grind one end sharp, and fasten the other into the ivory end of the spear. The iron will keep sharp much longer than the ivory, and therefore is more useful; besides which, they can sharpen it again, upon a stone, more easily than they can ivory.

I had been told that they were very dishonest, and that I must be careful not to give up the needles, or whatever it might be, until I had received what I was to have in exchange; but I did not find this to be the case. Once or twice I handed down the needles, and the man took them, but when he had examined them, he was not satisfied, and handed them back again. After some time, I had only three left, when I saw a piece of white bear-skin, which I thought would make a comfortable mat for my berth. I held these up, and pointed to the skin. The man was not satisfied, and held up four fingers and pointed. I ran down and brought up some more, and offered the four. But now he kept the skin, and held up four fingers and his thumb. I shook my head, and held up the four fingers of one hand, and the four needles in the other, and said—"No, no," though I don't suppose he was much wiser for this. He then called one of his neighbours, and there was a long consultation, which ended in his handing up the skin, and receiving the four needles, for which we had originally agreed.

On another occasion they were successful cheats;

but it was in a different way. When they catch a seal, they often skin it entire, and then sew up the slit they have made, and also the holes formed by its short arms and legs, and only leave a hole in the neck. When they tie a string round this, they can blow up the skin like a bladder, and it looks just like a dried seal again. The sailors call these "Dans," and buy some of them for foot-balls to be used upon the ice. It must be confessed, that a foot-ball three feet long, and above a foot thick, is not a very convenient size; but this does not much matter to Jack. The Esquimaux fill these dans with seal or whale oil, and bring it to the ships for sale. One year two ships happened to be together, and they had sold some of these dans full of oil to one of them. They made signs that they wished for the skins back again, so the oil was emptied into barrels, and they were returned. There was a good deal of ice about at the time, and as soon as they had received them, they went behind a high piece, and filled them with water. Then they went to the other ship, and offered them for sale as skins full of oil. As no trick was suspected, they were bought; but this time they did not ask to have the skins returned, and the fraud was not discovered until some time after, when they were emptied, in order that all the oil might be put together.

The Esquimaux seem to be very strong, though they are short. I regret that I did not measure any of them, but they were certainly not more than five feet high. Many, indeed, are less than this. They have cheerful, good-tempered looking faces. Their skin is of a yellowish olive colour, and their hair is generally black. I only saw one man who had a few grey hairs — and he was evidently old. Their hair is generally very rough, and hanging about in all directions, but some of them have it smooth, and tied up into a knot on the top of the head. Sometimes they wear upon this a little hat about three inches in diameter, made of coarse grass, but usually they have nothing but the hood of their jackets. They are generally entirely without beard or whiskers. I only saw one man who had a few straggling hairs on his chin, and he was the same whose hair was grey. There is one thing about them which can never be mistaken, as the ship smells most offensively for a week at least after they have been on board. Their usual dress consists of a jacket, trousers, and boots made of seal-skin, with the hair remaining on. The jacket fits close to the body, and is made with a hood; so that they can put this over their head, and when seated in their canoes, if the water were washing over them all day, they would not get wet. The sailors often buy these jackets from them, for they are very warm, and wear well when cut up and made into waistcoats. The first thing to be done, is to tie them to a piece of string and throw them overboard, so that they may be dragged through the sea after the ship for a few days; then they are hung up in the rigging every fine day, and even on wet ones, to see if the wind and rain and sun will take away the scent; but all is in vain. The man cuts them up, and makes his waistcoat; but he has generally worn it a long time before it entirely loses its smell. Sometimes these seal-skins are very handsome, being

c 3

mottled with black and grey hair, and they ornament them by tying teeth to the bottom of the jacket. I have seen above a hundred teeth fastened to one jacket. Their clothes are sometimes made of deer-skin, instead of seal-skin.

They seem to be almost insensible to cold. It happened that the night they came off to us was fine and tolerably warm ; but even when cold and snowing they act in the same way, selling all their clothes off their backs. If anything was offered for which they wished, they did not hesitate to part with their jacket, trousers and boots ; and many thus stripped, remained several hours paddling about the ship. Indeed they stayed until after one o'clock in the morning, and had then to return to their island, which was several miles distant. They always come off at night, and seldom go out hunting or fishing except at this time. The reason is, that the snow and ice are so dazzling by day, as almost to blind them, on which account they wear a very simple protection made of a piece of wood cut into the shape of a pair of spectacles; but instead of having glass there is a long horizontal slit, about an eighth of an inch deep, through which they can see sufficiently to shoot, or to direct their course, whilst they still avoid the great glare of the snow.

They do not appear to like fires or cooked victuals. One year when one of them came on board soon after dinner, the captain desired the cook to offer him some pea-soup, which was still hot. The man took the basin, and then returned it without tasting it. The captain, thinking that perhaps he did not know what was to be done with it, took a mouthful; but having just dined he did not wish to swallow it, and therefore spit it out again. The man took the basin, and following his example took a mouthful, and then very gravely spit it out upon the deck. I noticed some pieces of blubber in their canoes when they came off to us, with which they would much sooner refresh themselves than with pea-soup. One year whilst about the ship, they saw a seal lying upon a piece of ice at a little distance. They started off; caught it; killed it; skinned it; ate it; and returned to the ship in little more than a quarter of an hour; but I mention this from report, not having been with the ship at the time. They are very rarely seen but in their canoes, by the crews of these vessels.

CHAPTER II.

Leaving the Esquimaux, we sailed up the Strait for two or three days, and now began to meet with a good deal of difficulty from the quantity of ice we encountered. It was at this time that we first found the advantage of our ice-chocks, and the double bottom of the ship, for she now began to give and receive many heavy blows. One unaccustomed to it would think that the ship could not possibly proceed amongst the large masses which lie in every direction around her. This is the most difficult time for the men at the wheel, and steering the ship is now such hard work, that I have often known them in a violent perspiration, even during a cold night, though they had no clothing but their common sailor's jacket. Whilst among the ice, it is necessary to have one or two people constantly looking out, and the most opposite directions are given to the steersman every few minutes, according to the position of the pieces of ice. Perhaps there is a large piece just a-head, and the man forward cries out "starboard," which means, make the ship go to the left hand. Then in a minute or two comes "larboard," or make the ship go to the right hand; and before she can have her course changed, she strikes against a large piece, which shakes everything in the ship, and makes all the bells ring in the cabin, and upon deck.

We think that we are getting on very well, and that a small piece of ice which we can just see above the water is of no consequence, and that we will strike against that and force it out of the way. But when we have struck it, we find that it is a very large heavy piece almost entirely under water, which prevents her from moving forward; and now comes the order,—"Shiver the main-sail," which means, alter the sails in such a way, that the wind instead of blowing behind them, shall blow in front, and so force the ship backwards instead of forwards, until she is free from the piece of ice. And so we go on all the day. But night is the time when the ship receives the hardest blows; for sometimes it is too dark to see the pieces in the way, and so she sails right upon them. At first there is something very uncomfortable, when lying fast asleep, in being awoke by a shock, which almost shakes you out of the bed, and the next moment hearing a noise passing just under your head, as if all the planks in the ship's side were being torn up, the cause of which is, that she has struck upon a piece of ice, and cut it in two by the blow, and each portion slides scraping along the sides, until she has passed it.

At length the ice becomes so thick and close that the ship cannot advance; she has struck upon a piece and cannot move—you try to go backwards, but no, the ice has closed in, and there you are completely fast. You hope to be at liberty again in a short time, from some change in the wind; but the wind either does not change, or if it does, the ice does not open. You now look out for some large iceberg, and with long poles push away the ice just under the bows, and force your way towards it. Or if the ice is becoming thicker, you do not wish to be quite blocked up, but make fast to the first iceberg, or large flat piece that will answer the purpose, which is very easily done. A man is let down over the ship's side, or drops from her bowsprit upon the ice, and runs upon it to a little distance. Here he makes a hole in the ice with a pick-axe, about a foot or eighteen inches deep, into which he puts one end of an ice anchor, which is a piece of wrought iron made into the form of a capital Roman S; one end is slipped into the hole, and, a rope being tied to the opposite end, is made fast to the ship. I have seen her fastened in this way with five anchors to a single piece, and they were all got out of the holes, and she was under weigh again, in about five minutes after the ice began to open.

The object in anchoring thus is to save the ship from the blows which she might receive from the loose pieces striking against her. The iceberg now receives the shock of these pieces, and keeps her quite snug and safe. But there is another very important advantage derived from it. We cannot get fresh water whilst at sea, and if the voyage is a long one, or if there are many people on board, this begins to be scarce. Now in summer there are always pools of water upon the tops of the icebergs, or of flat high pieces, even though they may not deserve this name; and this water is generally perfectly fresh and good. It is formed partly from the melting of the snow and ice upon the upper surface of the berg, and partly by the rain, which is collected in the little hollows. Some people even say, that salt water never freezes, and that the whole of the ice is therefore fresh; but though generally the case, this is not entirely true. I have often frozen salt water, and the water found upon the ice is sometimes salt, though this is not often the case. As soon then as the ship is made fast, the ice presents a very busy scene. Two or three men remain in the ship to haul up the buckets and empty them into the tanks, and the rest are continually going backwards and forwards to fill them at these fresh-water pools, and bring them to the ship.

As soon as the tanks are filled, the men are at liberty to amuse themselves as they like best; which they always do by playing at two games well known to all schoolboys—baste the bear and football. The football is, it must be confessed, rather larger and heavier than most schoolboys would like to use, for it is often two or three feet long, being made of a dried seal's-skin blown out; —the dan, which I before described—with which they take care to provide themselves when the Esquimaux come to the ship.

It is not quite so easy playing upon an iceberg as it is upon firm ground, and many a fall the sailors get when they think that they are going to give the dan a hearty kick. Though not so smooth as ice upon a pond, it is even more slippery. The surface of an iceberg most nearly resembles a very small island, with many little hills and hollows, covered over with snow, but having some small ponds or lakes in different parts, which are not frozen. The hills are formed partly by droppings from the rocks, under which the berg is forming, and partly by the snow drifting after it has fallen, and the players are thus almost always going either up or down hill on a slide. One is almost tempted to envy the white bear's broad yielding foot, which does not slip on the ice. We saw the mark of one very distinctly upon a small iceberg, to which we one day anchored. It appeared as if the piece had broken in two, and he had probably sailed away upon the other portion.

We do not meet with many white bears; the greatest number I have seen at once was four upon one very large iceberg, several miles long; but two of them were so far off, that they could only be seen with a telescope. They make a hole large enough to lie down in near the edge of the berg, and it is easy to see who has been there, by the brown colour which the snow acquires from their sleeping in it.

The animals we most frequently saw were seals, which are tolerably numerous. They do not look very intelligent, but they have sufficient sense for their peculiar station in life, and also make use of it; which is as much as can be said of many beings, who are held in much higher estimation. The enemy they have most to fear is the white bear; and, in order to avoid him, they always lie close to a hole in the piece of ice. As soon then as they hear or see anything of their foe, they pop through this hole into the sea, and Master Bruin must wait patiently for another chance. On a fine day we often saw them lying basking thus in the sun for a long time together. In winter they do not forget their precaution of lying near the hole; but then they have another enemy, who is more successful than our friend the bear. When the snow falls it covers them over, and soon becomes frozen, so as to stick together, and form a shelter, under which the seal lies snug and warm, or, at any rate, comfortable, in a seal's sense of the word. The Esquimaux then go out to hunt them, and take their dogs with them. These run about upon the ice, until they come to the part beneath which a seal is lying. Here they begin to scratch, and the Esquimaux comes to help them. He soon makes a hole through the ice, and finds his prey very quietly composed, and expecting no callers in such unseasonable weather. I do not know whether the cold makes them drowsy or not, but, at any rate, they do not escape through their original hole into the water, and so are caught. The man keeps the skin and flesh for his own use, and gives the offal to the dogs on the spot, which are then in good spirits to set off again and search for another. In this way the hunter will often kill several seals in a single day.

They have a curious appearance when swimming, all that is visible being a round black head, which moves on at a quick rate through the water, and which, when fired upon, instantly disappears. The part where they are most numerous is in Davis' Straits. Sometimes when whales are scarce, the fishermen catch seals instead, and they reckon a thousand of these animals to be equal to one whale. Occasionally they are so numerous, that they appear almost to cover the ice; and the sailors go upon it, and with a small heavy bludgeon strike one as hard as they can just above its nose, or on its forehead, and then go to another, which they treat in the same way. When they have thus stunned all that do not escape, they take long knives and skin them as quickly as possible, cut off the blubber, and leave them, sometimes, in their haste, even before they are quite dead. The colour of the young is very different from that of the old ones, being a golden yellow; whilst the old ones are gray or mottled, like a common hair trunk. It is with seal's-skins that these trunks are principally covered.

From the appearance of the ice as it closed around us, when we made fast to the iceberg, we expected to be blocked up for some time; and the next morning nothing was to be seen from the deck but ice in every direction. I went up to the mast-head, in hopes of being more successful there; but still the same scene, bounded only by fog, which was becoming thicker: and in this state we went to dinner. Whilst we were below, however, the wind changed, and in about half an hour the ice began to open; in an hour we had taken up our anchors, and set the sails; and in three or four hours from the time when we could see no water, there was scarcely a piece of ice remaining in sight. It is very curious to notice what a sudden and remarkable change an hour or two sometimes effects, a slight change in the wind, or the turn of the tide often making the ice disappear as if by magic.

In the afternoon of this day, as we were sailing quietly along, a man in the fore-top said he saw

Google

a sail at some distance. We had parted company with our consort, the Prince Albert, before entering the Strait, and had not seen her for a fortnight. We had lost sight of each other in a fog, just before encountering the first ice. She had been more fortunate then we were, by keeping further to the north, and had entered the Strait during a temporary gleam of clear weather, whilst we, being further to the south, had been detained for four days by contrary wind and fog; during which we durst not attempt to enter it. It was very well that we did not attempt it, for as we have seen, we had been carried by currents nearly sixty miles out of our reckoning, and should probably have struck upon some of the land on the south coast. When, however, we came in sight of her again, she was blocked up by ice, and presented a most singular appearance; for she looked as if she were standing upon her mast ends in the ice, whilst her shadow was visible in the water, which appeared to be just at its edge. I saw her first without a telescope, and thought I must surely be mistaken; but when I got the glass I saw her so distinctly that I could make out what sails she had set, though, when we afterwards compared notes, we found that she was about *twelve* miles distant from us at the time. This inverted appearance of objects is not very uncommon in high latitudes; and we are often very much deceived by what looks like land or vessels, even when they have their natural position.

One afternoon the clouds assumed such an appearance of land, and retained it steadily for so long a time, that they were entered in the log-book as being Queen Anne's Foreland, which is land upon the north coast. The atmosphere is so heavy in consequence of the cold, and so full of fogs, that it seems almost to become a sort of mirror, in which objects are reflected when the light falls upon it in a particular way; so that the real ship or iceberg is the one in the water, whilst the one in the sky is merely its image, though this sometimes appears the more distinct of the two. In consequence also of the air being so thick and cold, objects seem to be raised much higher than they really are; so that we can see them at a greater distance than we could do if the air were lighter. This effect of "refraction" is very curious, and may be easily shown by a simple basin of water, and a half-crown, or anything which is put into the bottom of it. If we take an empty basin, and put into it a piece of money, and remove to such a distance as just to lose sight of it, and then pour in water very gently, so as not to move it, we shall see it quite plainly, though it still lies at the bottom where it did. It looks as if it were raised up by the water. Now the same thing occurs in the cold heavy atmosphere of the northern seas, and the land appears raised, so that we can see it sometimes at a great distance.

Hudson's Strait and Bay are, however, very liable to thick fogs, so that it is frequently impossible to see further than from one end of the ship to the other. Besides the inconvenience and danger of sailing when the weather is so thick, the fog or cold produces another curious effect. It seems to find its way into the compass-boxes, and to make the compasses sluggish, and as it were unwilling to move.

You never can be sure when you look at the compass that it is pointing truly, for sometimes you may turn it round a sixteenth or more, without its moving. It will be easily seen how much this is by looking at the sketch of the compass, which is divided into thirty-two points, as they are called; so that a sixteenth would be two of these points. In order to remedy this, the man at the wheel has a thin piece of wood, with which he keeps touching the compass-box, so as to shake it a little, and then the needle will move. But if he forgets to do this, he may be steering quite in a wrong direction, though the compass remains the same. It appears to be owing either to the cold or the damp, for the compass which is in the cabin, where there is generally a fire, swings round nearly as usual, though even it is more or less affected.

But there is another difficulty which is much greater than this, and not so easily remedied. As we approach to the North Pole, the variation of the compass increases. Suppose we examine a compass in England, and see how it points, and call this north, because the magnet is said to point to the north, we should not be strictly correct. Instead of pointing to the north, it really points nearly north-north-west, or N.N.W. as it is marked on the compass; but as we go further north and more towards the west, it points still further and further away from the north, until, in some parts of Hudson's Strait, it points west-north-west, W.N.W.

Indeed there is a place in Davis' Strait where it actually points south-east, S.E. Now if this was always the case, and with all compasses, it would be of little consequence, as allowance could easily be made for it; but the misfortune is, that it does not affect all compasses alike. There is an island at the entrance to Hudson's Bay, called Mansfield, where this difference is the most remarkable. When ships are near this place, there are always two compasses placed side by side for the man to steer by; besides these there is one in the cabin, and often another is placed somewhere near the middle of the ship. Now one would think that these ought all to point alike, but instead of that, one of those by which the man is steering may be pointing north, and the other north-west; the one in the cabin is perhaps pointing north by east, and the one towards the middle of the ship north-north-west. Now which is to be relied on? By which is the man to steer? Another very curious thing is, that if the ship's course is altered, all of them will often agree again, though she may be just in the same place, but simply have her head directed a different way. On one occasion, during a fog, they differed so much that the captain had two brought down into the cabin, and placed on opposite sides of the table, when one needle pointed east, the other west, at the same time. Of course nothing could be done; so he "hove the ship to," or arranged the sails in such a way, that, whilst some of them were blowing her forwards, the others were blowing her backwards; and by this means she did not move until morning, when it became clear, and he could see land, and know by it how to steer.

This effect upon the needle continues for nearly a degree from Mansfield Island, so that it would appear as if there was some local attraction in it.

Perhaps there are large iron mines near the surface, but it is not known, for it has never been examined. It is a long low island, which is in most parts very little above the water, and has some small trees upon it.

The ship one year almost formed a nearer acquaintance with it than she wished. She was sailing in such a direction, according to the compass, that she ought to have been going nearly parallel with the end of it. There was a thick fog. When the fog, which was very thick, cleared away, they were so near the island, as to see the breakers distinctly upon the shore, from which they were not above two or three miles distant. In about half an hour more the ship would probably have struck, for she was sailing straight upon it.

How truly may it be said of those who "go down to the sea" in these ships, "These see the works of the Lord, and His wonders in the deep!" They have to sail amongst icebergs, high enough and heavy enough to sink them almost in a moment, if they struck: they have to sail amongst rocks which descend so perpendicularly, that when the bowsprit is almost touching them, there are above one hundred fathoms of water; there are no friendly light-houses upon these rocks to warn them of their danger, and to show them how to steer; and they have to sail through fogs so thick that they often cannot see the head of the ship from the stern; in long dark and dreary nights, when their best friend, the compass, forsakes them, and sometimes, as it were, even cheats them into dangers. And besides all these things, there are currents so strong that the ships can hardly make head against them. Once near the east end of Charles's Island, about fifteen miles distant, we appeared to be sailing three or four knots an hour all day, and the next day at noon found that we were only five miles distant from where we were the previous noon. We had sailed nearly ninety miles, and the current had carried us back above eighty. One of the ships went one year to Ungava Bay, which is near the entrance of Hudson's Strait, upon the south coast, and sailed down part of the coast during the night. In the morning the Captain was amazed and alarmed by his position. He was in the midst of rocks reaching as high as the top of the masts. He had sailed over their summits at high water; and the tide fell above one hundred feet, and left him amongst them; and here the tide often runs eight or nine knots an hour. And yet there has not been an accident of importance to any of them for above fifty years, nor do I remember to have heard of any of them having been lost at sea. May we not then exclaim — "Oh! that men would, therefore, praise the Lord for His goodness, and declare the wonders that He doeth for the children of men!"

After leaving the Strait, we sailed across the Bay for York Factory, where we were going to receive our cargo of furs, and buffalo-tallow, and hides, which are the principal produce of the country. For a day or two before we reached our anchorage the water began to be very green, and not the deep blue to which we had been so long accustomed. And now we began to have summer visitors: for a few butterflies, and one or two dragon-flies, came to the ship, and the weather became warm and comfortable again. Now we began to enjoy being upon the deck in the pleasant sun, and threw off some of the extra clothing which we had worn in the Straits. Though we passed through them in July and August, it did not seem like summer, for we had fires in the cabin, which were very necessary for comfort, and generally wore our great coats also during the day.

It generally happens that two or three times each voyage the ship becomes for some hours unmanageable, in consequence of the cold. The fog settles upon the rigging and freezes there, and the ropes become so thickly covered with ice that they will not run through the blocks or pulleys. When the sun comes out in the day-time, the ice falls down upon the deck and requires the crew to keep a good look out, that it does not fall upon their heads.

As soon as the sea began to look green, which it only does in shallow water, every body was on the look-out for land, and many were the fruitless journeys to the top of the mast.

At length appeared the tops of the trees, like little specks, standing out of the water, in the horizon; and then we saw the green colour from the grass, which came down to the water's edge; and we thought we had never seen any grass look so fresh, and bright, and beautiful before; for we had seen nothing but sea, and ice, and barren, black rocks, covered with snow, for many weeks. We soon came to the mouth of York River, where we were to lie, and cast anchor about nine o'clock in the morning. We fired five guns, that they might hear us at the Factory or Fort; and we thought that we were very much pleased to be at the end of our voyage, about which we had talked so much. And yet when the small vessel came alongside which was to take us on shore, we felt almost unwilling to go. We had been so long on board, that the ship had become as it were an old friend, and we felt it as a home. We were accustomed to its rolling motion, and we had insensibly become attached to our berths and our furniture. We knew each other; and though we could not walk a hundred yards in any direction, what did that matter? we had the fresh air around us, the open sky above us, and the boundless sea beneath us. And knowing that we went a hundred miles or more each day through it, we did not feel as if confined, but seemed to have complete liberty. But when we went on shore, we felt homeless and desolate; we did not know whom we should meet; we did not know how we should be entertained; we were leaving our familiar scenes and our daily occupations, and though we were pleased to reach our place of destination, our pleasure was a good deal mingled with sadness.

CHAPTER III.

York Factory or Fort is built upon the bank of York River, about seven miles from its mouth; and is in Lat. 57° N.; which is very nearly the same as that of Stromness. The river is very broad, but so shallow, that the ship cannot go up to the Factory, but lies in the roads, at its mouth. The cargo is discharged, and the goods for England brought down in small schooners, which do not draw above seven or eight feet of water.

This is the general character of most of the rivers which empty themselves into Hudson's Bay. York River is from two to three miles broad at its mouth; and as far as it retains this name, which it does for about forty or fifty miles, it continues three or four times the breadth of the Thames at London Bridge, and in several parts it is much wider. There are many rapids, and it is generally shallow. North, or Nelson River, which enters the Bay nearly at the same place, is so wide at its mouth, and for a few miles above it, that the shore on the opposite side is not visible. It is also very full of rapids, and, in fact, is not navigable. The same broad, shallow character occurs at Moose, a factory on Moose River, James's Bay, Hudson's Bay. The ship cannot come within ten miles of this factory in consequence of the numerous shoals.

It is not difficult, in some degree, to account for this. Though the latitude of York is the same as that of Stromness, and the latitude of Moose the same as that of London, yet the climate is exceedingly different. The winter commences about the beginning or middle of October, with a heavy fall of snow, which lies upon the ground for a few days, and is accompanied with severe frost, so that the rivers are covered with ice. Then the weather becomes warm again for about a fortnight; the snow melts, the ice disappears, and the rivers are again open. This is called the second summer; and occurs in some other countries besides Hudson's Bay. In Russia it is as regular as the other seasons; and is there called "Meninka Summer," which is the Russian diminutive, and means "Little Summer." After the ships have been frozen up in the harbour of Cronstadt, the ice breaks up, and the hot weather returns for a short time, so as to enable them to leave. If they do not avail themselves of this opportunity, the ice forms again, and they are set fast until the next spring.

The winter then, in Hudson's Bay, sets in about, or soon after, the end of October, in good earnest, and continues until May. During the whole of this time, the ground is covered with snow, and the rivers are fast with ice; the Bay, also, is nearly, if not entirely, frozen up. The cold is so severe, that the thermometer frequently stands at 40° below zero; and the banks of the river upon which York stands are so thoroughly cooled, that in digging two or three feet below the surface, even in summer, you come to frozen ground. The heat is proportionably great in summer, and the thermometer often stands at 90° in the shade.

When the summer does begin, the progress of vegetation is rapid. The leaves quickly cover the trees, and the country around looks beautifully green, from the sudden growth of the long, rich, marshy grass, which is found upon the banks and shores of the Bay. Whilst we were at York, which was in August and September, we were eating well-grown mustard and cress, which had only been sown four days before; and fresh venison, which had been killed the previous October, and kept in ice the whole time, though it must be confessed that it was beginning to be rather highly flavoured.

When the spring commences, the ice breaks up in the rivers, and in so doing, often breaks and carries down with it large portions of the banks, which consist of clay or sand. The mud thus formed, collects at the mouth of the rivers where the current is less rapid, and thus a continual process of widening goes on, whilst, at the same time, they become more shallow. Sometimes the breaking up of the ice is very frightful. If the river remains closed below longer than it does above, the ice is carried down with great force, and becomes piled in immense blocks upon and under the surface of the ice below, and rises to a great height. If the banks are not very high, or if they are disposed to break, the ice tears them up, and overwhelms the country, uprooting and carrying away with it trees, houses, and everything that is in its way.

York Factory stands upon a bank between twenty and thirty feet above the river, but one year there was extreme danger from the accumulation of ice a little above it. The alarm was given one night, by ringing the large alarm-bell, that it had actually begun to sweep over the bank, and all the people rushed out of their houses, half-dressed, in the utmost fear. Had the danger proved real, probably no one would have remained to tell the tale. All would, no doubt, have been swept away by the descending ice and water. As it happened, however, it was only a small piece, which, having broken off, had fallen upon the bank, and given rise to the opinion that the whole mass was coming down. In a day or two the ice broke up at the mouth of the river, and all was hurried into the sea, without having occasioned any damage.

The situation of York Factory is anything but attractive. It is so near the Bay, that it is subject to great and sudden changes of weather. In the morning it is sometimes so hot that only light summer clothing can be worn, and in the afternoon a breeze may spring up from the north or north-east, and bring such a cold fog with it, that warm winter garments are essential. The country surrounding it is all marsh and swamp, so that you cannot walk half a mile in any direction without sinking up to the ankles or knees, and the ground upon which it is built is so marshy, that flowers grow within the gates which are considered peculiarly bog-flowers in England. It is built entirely of wood, and forms two quadrangles about one hundred yards long. The front quadrangle has only three sides, as the place of the fourth is supplied by the river, which runs in front of it. A long platform runs from the centre of the furthest side down to the river, and ends in a sort of quay, upon which the goods may be landed.

A raised wooden platform runs in front of each side, upon which you are obliged to walk in wet weather, and which is preferable even in dry.

The front quadrangle is composed of warehouses, packing-shops, the store-house, which is a large building in the centre, the mess-room, and the house in which any gentlemen coming to the factory on business lodge during their stay. The back one consists of the commandant's house, or chief-trader, as his real title is, the office, and the different work-shops and houses of the labourers. There is a garden in the centre of the front quadrangle, but nothing grows in it except a little cress and some lettuce, which consists of four or five small leaves ; no turnips or potatoes will grow, and the commandant's lady told me that sometimes a few onions were sent as a treat from Red River, which is five or six hundred miles in the interior of the country.

The trees around the factory are pines, willows, birches, and poplars, but they are very small and stunted. In walking among them you can see over them in many places, and though the ground is covered with trees, yet they have to go five miles from the factory before they can find any worth cutting for fire-wood. To this place the furs are brought in the spring, and are here re-packed and warehoused until the ship comes once a year to take them away.

It may be readily supposed, that there is not much society. There are, perhaps in all, forty or fifty persons, and in summer there are besides a few wigwams without the gates, in which some Indian families live. The chief-trader, his wife, the surgeon, and one or two clerks are the regular residents. The remaining number consists of labourers, and their wives and families. At different periods of the year, the number is increased by gentlemen who come down from forts, or "houses," in different parts of the country with furs. It is to these places in the interior that the Indians bring the furs, from whence they are brought down to York, as soon as the rivers are sufficiently free from ice to admit the passage of the boats, which is the only mode of conveyance, as roads and carriages are unknown.

Whilst we remained at York, I had an opportunity of accompanying Mr. —— a few hundred miles up the country, who was going to take charge of a house about a six weeks' journey from York. Our company consisted of Mr. ——; Lawrènce Basîl, a Canadian, our steersman; and Bïdòu, another Canadian, our bowsman. There were, besides, ten of the labourers whom we had brought out from Orkney, and myself.

Our travelling furniture was very simple. A large piece of oil-cloth, two blankets, and a buffalo's hide tanned with the hair on, furnished bed and bedding. Sheets are articles unknown in this country, for summer and winter the inhabitants lie between blankets, which is rather a luxury than a privation when you become accustomed to them. A basket containing buffalo tongues, hams, pork, and biscuit was provided for our entertainment, and the men were furnished with as much pimmikin, or pimmocan, as would serve them for the journey. This is a very useful diet, and consists of buffalo's suet and tallow melted together, and made stiff by dried buffalo meat grated into it; it is then poured into a bag made of buffalo's hide sewn up, and capable of holding about a hundred-weight. When wanted for use, a lump is chopped off with a hatchet, and eaten raw. It looks something like very common plum-pudding, and eats a little like a candle flavoured with coarse sand.

What is called gentleman's or fine pimmikin, is made of buffalo marrow, dried meat, and a kind of black berry, which grows in abundance in the woods. At first it is disagreeable from its greasy taste, and the marrow melting in the mouth and leaving the meat; but this is soon overcome, and it is then really not at all unpalatable, especially when eaten with sugar. Besides these things, we had a keg of butter, a small quantity of wine and brandy, a tent rolled up and stowed away in the boat, a couple of hatchets, and flint and steel, with some common touchwood. In the boat were also the bales of goods which were going into the country for the winter's use.

As is generally the case, the guide, or steersman, and the bowsman were drunk before setting off. A small quantity of spirits is always given them the day before, to last them during the journey; but this is usually finished before starting.

When we set off the wind was fair for going up the river, so we fixed our mast, and set our sail. Any one who has been accustomed to boating at home, would share the dismay with which one of the Orkney lads, who had been a sailor, exclaimed—" And is that what you call a mast?" In truth, it required some degree of courtesy to give it this name A small pine tree had been cut down, probably that morning, and the branches lopped off, but the bark remained ; the thick end was thrust into a hole in the bottom of the boat, and the thin end was the top of the mast. But though the entire tree, it was too short for our boat, so that the whole of the sail could not be hoisted. It is not the custom to use a sail much, and no provision is made for fastening the sail-ropes or "sheets." To supply this deficiency, the oars were laid across the boat, and when the ropes were fastened, the men were desired to sit upon them, and keep them in their places.

We soon came to a turn in the river which deprived us of any further assistance from the wind, when Mr. Lawrènce lowered the sail, took it from the mast and oars, and, with the most perfect coolness, hove the former overboard. In this he showed more judgment than I, at first, imagined ; the mast would have been heavy and inconvenient in the boat; we were travelling the whole time through woods ; consequently, if we should ever again want one, we could pull to the bank, cut down a tree, strip off its branches, and in ten minutes have as good a one, at any rate, as that which we had lost.

We soon came to the first shallow place in the river, which is but a short distance from the factory, but even before arriving here our steersman began to sober himself. It is true his method, though efficacious, was not entirely voluntary. In coming down a rapid almost everything depends upon the skill of the steersman, and he cannot alter the course of the boat quickly enough to avoid the rocks and stones which lie in the way, by means of a common rudder. They always steer, therefore, with a long oar, or sweep, fastened to the boat's stern, with a single stroke of which they can turn her almost half round. In order to use this, they must stand upon a raised platform instead of sitting. Now, although Mr. Lawrènce had a sort of notion that it was desirable to keep upon his legs, yet he was not entirely able to put it into practice; and, before we had been long on our journey, the sweep had the control of itself, whilst its master, having fallen overboard, was floundering about in the river, trying to regain his balance. Fortunately the water was not deep, and the only effect of this manœuvre, which was repeated about twenty times in the course of the day, was to cool his skin, to damp his clothes, and restore him to some degree of sobriety. Whether Bîdoù's head was stronger or his allowance less, I cannot say, but he did manage to keep his position in the bow of the boat.

We passed the first shallow pretty well, as the bottom of the boat did not stick, though it touched the ground. But the second was more troublesome. The season had been unusually dry, the water was uncommonly low, and the boat was rather deep with thirteen men in it. At length it stuck fast, and the oars were of no avail to get it off again. Nothing remained but to lighten it, which did not require a thought on the part of the Canadians, who were old "voyageurs," and accustomed to it. They at once jumped into the river, and exhorted the Orkney men to follow their example, in such a mixture of Canadian, French, and English oaths and encouragements, as experience had taught them was most useful, or as the necessity of the moment supplied. The Scotchmen, however, did not understand this sort of extempore footbath, and hesitated; but there was no alternative, so at length over the side they all went, some jumping, some still hanging on, and others lowering themselves very carefully, so as to wet their clothes as little as possible, for taking them off would have been ridiculous, and even turning up the trowsers was a superfluous precaution.

And now when the boat was thus lightened, and every man put his shoulder under it and pushed it along, it was soon over the shallow, and in deep water again, and all scrambled into it as they best could. This plan was repeated several times during the day with success, and at length the men thought nothing of it, but jumped into the water, as soon as they felt the bottom touch the ground. At last, however, even this failed us. The river was divided by a small island, covered with wood, which lay in the middle of it, and we took the channel on the right side. We soon stuck fast; got ourselves clear; stuck fast again, and were again cleared; and had advanced so far, that we could see the channel on the other side the island, when we again struck. And now everybody was in the water, and we pushed, and pulled, and lifted and carried the boat up the rapid; but to no purpose. Every step we took the water became shallower, and the boat consequently more difficult to move; and at length, after trying nearly an hour, we were forced to give it up in despair. We turned her round, and came down the river to try

by Google

P. 48.

Digitized by Google

the channel on the other side of the island. We found this deep and good, and soon gained the undivided river again, having been two hours in accomplishing a mile and a half, which was about the length of the island.

About seven o'clock we came to a smooth slope on the bank of the river, covered with grass, and having plenty of wood above it; and here, as it was the first day, and the men were new at the work, and tired, Mr. —— decided to stay for the night. We had had a pretty hard day's work of ten hours, and had come nine miles from the factory. The first thing to be done was to light a fire, and the next to cook our supper; so whilst some of the men were bringing the things out of the boat, the others were cutting down trees, or collecting dried wood upon the bank, and in a few minutes there was a bright, blazing, crackling fire.

Near the place where we stopped was a little creek, surrounded with long grass and rushes, and here we saw some wild ducks feeding. Whilst the men were making the fire, and putting up the tent, Mr. —— and I took our guns and crept through the long grass until we came within shot. One duck was killed, and another wounded, but it escaped into the grass on the opposite side. It seemed a pity not to try and get it, so tucking up my trowsers, I waded across, but the precaution might have been omitted, for they were quickly wet through when the water became deeper. I remained until quite dusk, and then returned to the tent, with two or three ducks and an owl. Tired with the day's work, and wet through, it was very pleasant to sit in the tent in front of the long bright fire, and enjoy the supper of tea and buffalo tongue, which had been prepared whilst I was away. Bidoù was our cook, for all Canadians are expert in the culinary art. He had spread a napkin upon the grass, and upon this was laid the teapot, with the plates and knives and forks. The men had made themselves a mess, called "rubbaboo," and were sitting round the fire enjoying themselves. This consists of flour, water, and pimmikin. When they have flour, which was given to them before leaving York, they heat a large kettle full of water, and when it boils they put in lumps of pimmikin, and stir it up till the grease is melted; they then stir in a quantity of flour, and the whole forms a dish a good deal like oatmeal porridge in appearance, though I cannot say that it resembles it much in taste.

When we had finished supper, our beds were made ready in the tent. The oilcloth was laid upon the ground to keep off wet; the buffalos' hide, or robe as it is called, was laid upon this, and formed the mattrass; and the blankets were spread upon the top. I took an old French soldier's knapsack with me, which had been my companion in most parts of England, Wales, and Ireland, and this made an excellent pillow, and my great coat served as a pillow-case. Taking off our wet clothes was out of the question, for they were all we had with us. They dried as much as they could whilst we were standing before the fire, and then we lay down beneath our blankets, and were soon as fast asleep as if on the softest bed. Each of the men had a blanket with him, and rolling themselves up in these, they lay down round the fire, or under the bushes, or wherever they thought they should be most comfortable.

During the night it rained very heavily, and blew hard, and as our tent had not been well pitched, the wind soon blew part of it loose, and allowed the rain to enter. We arose before it was full daylight to proceed on our journey, and I had the comfort to find that my waistcoat and shoes were water-proof, for the pockets of the former were full of water when I took it up, and the latter had most faithfully kept all the rain which had fallen into them during the night.

The country through which we were travelling was very unpicturesque; the banks were in many places high, but neither bold nor beautiful, and consist of clay, which has a heavy, dull, lifeless appearance. They are covered with low trees of the same kind as those near York; and in many parts these have been burnt, and nothing but the naked blackened trunks remain. If the fire has not been recent the trees become bleached, and look like bare poles. It is not always easy to say how the fires originate, which are so common in these woods. I have been told that in a high wind two trees are frequently rubbed against each other until they take fire. Perhaps it is so, but I never met any one who had seen it commence in this way. When a fire is lighted, either for cooking or for the night, no one thinks of putting it out; and I think this is a much more probable cause. The wind rising a little would easily blow it up, until the grass or roots about it take fire, and if the season is dry, the trees would soon be kindled. We pitched our tent one night upon a small, bare patch of soft heathy ground, and before going to sleep we found that the ground was on fire, but, as it was only smouldering, and there was no wind, we trusted that it would not reach the tent before morning, and lay down as usual. These fires are of little consequence; for there are no inhabitants to be injured, and no use is made of the wood, unless when travelling as we were. We were always glad when we saw burnt wood about the place where we wished to stay, as it is dry and burns so much more quickly and brightly than the green trees. It is true that the fur-bearing animals are sometimes injured, and their resorts destroyed by a fire; but so selfish is human nature, that no one complains on account of their sufferings, but only of the loss of the skins.

It is very common for the banks to slip into the river, and carry the trees down with them, and in journeying up the rivers you are obliged frequently to turn out of the way on this account. There is a fall of this kind a short distance from York, called the Indian's grave. A party, consisting of two or three Indian families, had encamped amongst the trees upon the bank, not fearing any danger, when it suddenly slipped, and overwhelmed them in the fall. The banks become dry during the hot weather and crack, forming deep fissures; and when the rain falls it enters these crevices, and gradually finds its way under the bottom of the bank into the river, until the base becomes so loose and slippery that it cannot support the weight of the earth and trees, and all slide down together.

We had soon passed the part of the river in which the oars were of any use, and the only way in which we could proceed was by tracking the boat. The men have a broad strap, which is slipped over their shoulders, and the loose ends are fastened to a long rope, which is tied to the bow of the boat. This is a very slow and fatiguing method of travelling, for owing to the soft clayey character of the banks, the men sink up to their knees nearly every step. In this journey they generally have to track for four days, and they are supplied with four pairs each of Indian shoes, which it is expected they will wear out in an equal number of days.

These shoes, or mocassins, are not made of hard tanned leather, like English shoes, but of soft buffalo or deer skin. They look like a large wash-leather sock, which ties round the ankle, and have no separate soles. The common ones are not ornamented; but the finer sort are made very pretty, with needle or quill work. The Indians and Canadians who make them, work devices of all manner of known and unknown, natural and unnatural flowers, in silk or with porcupine quills, which they dye of various bright colours. These shoes are admirably adapted to the country. They save the feet from being cut or pricked in travelling through the woods, and do not get hard and cracked from being wet. After having been wet through, nothing is necessary but to wring them out, and when they are dry to rub them in the hands until they become

F

soft again. In winter English shoes cannot be worn on account of the cold. The feet would be frost-bitten immediately, and besides this they must be of such an immense size, to allow of the stockings which are necessary, that they would be inconveniently heavy. In winter the best plan is, not to wear stockings, but to make duffle socks. This is a sort of very thick, warm woollen cloth, like a thick blanket. It is generally cut into pieces a foot or eighteen inches square, and the foot being placed in the middle, the corners are folded over it. Three thicknesses of duffle, and perhaps a larger stocking over them to keep them from dropping off, and an Indian shoe large enough to hold them all, are generally sufficient to keep the feet warm and comfortable.

It was rather stupid sitting or lying all day in the boat, and being dragged along, so we generally walked upon the bank with our guns, a-head of the men. We were rather too early in the season for the wild ducks to be returning south, and did not see many; but we occasionally shot one or two, which made something fresh for our supper. The cookery is very simple. One afternoon, just before we encamped, I shot a duck, and in a few minutes afterwards, wanting one or two of its feathers, asked Mr. Bīdoū for it; but the bird was already plucked, and its feathers were then floating down the river. In an hour or two more it was put into the pot and boiled, along with a wild goose, a brace of partridges, and a buffalo tongue.

We were walking a-head of the boat the second day of our journey, when we came to a place which was suitable for stopping at, and as the evening was advanced we determined to go no further. The men were about a mile behind us, trying to get the boat up a rapid, and were hid from our sight by a bend in the river. We thought we would get the fire ready for them, that they might have no delay when they came up, and accordingly collected a number of burnt trees, and cut down some others, and had a magnificent blazing fire just as they turned the point of land, and saw what we were doing. We found that this gave them so much spirit, that we often adopted the same plan and walked on before, so as to be ready for them when they came up. In dry weather and with dry wood this is easily managed, but it requires a little more skill during heavy rain. An Indian or Canadian would lose almost anything rather than his fire-bag, or its substitute. He could live for some time without food, and even if he had lost his bow and arrows, or his gun, he would still contrive to snare some sort of game, or to kill partridges with a stick. But if he cannot get a fire he cannot cook his game when he has caught it, for he does not eat his meat raw like the Esquimaux, and he would soon be killed, at any rate in winter, by the cold.

The best material for kindling a fire is birch bark. It contains a large quantity of turpentine, or some highly inflammable juice, and blazes strongly. It is a common thing to carry a small piece of this bark in some part of the dress, where it will be kept dry. But there must be some dry wood, or the blaze will be of no use even when obtained. Now the outside of a tree or a log will be wet enough in rainy weather; but if it is of any tolerable thickness, the rain does not soak through it. Accordingly he cuts the log down to the centre with his hatchet, and holds himself over it, so as to protect it from the rain. He then cuts out a number of thin chips like matches, and having struck a spark upon a piece of fungus, which grows from the pine trees, and is used as touchwood, or upon a piece of birch bark, or dry grass, if he can obtain any, he covers this up in his hand, and blows upon it till he sees a small flame. Then he has his dry chips ready; he lays his burning bark or moss upon some of them, covers it very lightly with others, and puts on pieces gradually increasing in size, until the fire will bear logs or branches of trees; and he has a good fire in almost less time than it has taken to describe it.

But suppose he has lost his flint and steel, how is he to manage then? Why truly, he may be badly off. Whilst the bow and arrow were in use, he would supply his want in the following way. He would find two pieces of wood (a hard and a soft piece answer the best, but it is not of much consequence), and would twist his bowstring round one piece, and holding his bow in his hand would rub it very rapidly against the other until they took fire. Now that the use of the bow is almost lost, the gunpowder which is employed instead serves well in such a case. He would mix up a little gunpowder with some dry moss or grass, and rub them well together in his hands, and would then put some more powder into the pan of his gun, and holding this close over the mixed moss would fire it off. Some of the sparks falling upon it would set it on fire, and he has all that he wants.

After travelling for two or three days, we came to a place where the river changes its name. Two rivers meet, called Hill and Fox rivers, and together form that up which we had come. Hill river is the deepest; but Fox river is the broadest, and appears to be the direct continuation, or rather source of the one which we now left. Hill river joins it nearly at a right angle, and then takes a course very winding in its details, though straight upon the whole; resembling the progress of a snake, which moves straight forward, though with many curves in its body.

I was sleepy from the heat of the sun, and did not pay particular attention to the banks as we passed them, and when we had ascended about a couple of miles, we encamped for the night amongst the trees. As it was still early, and the sun had not set, I took my gun, after we had lighted our fire and pitched our tent, to go into the wood, and see if I could shoot some ducks or partridges. Mr. —— said, just as I was starting off, "Mind you don't lose yourself." "Oh! no fear," I replied, and set off. I noticed that the sun was behind me as I went, and the river was running towards me on my *left* hand, so I thought I should have nothing to do but come back towards the sun, and keep the river on my right hand in returning. I soon came to a marshy pool, surrounded with long grass, in which I thought there would most likely be wild ducks, but not seeing any I waded through it, and proceeded further.

F 3

I found no ducks, but hearing the peculiar cry of the wood partridge, or ptarmigan, I pressed on through the wood, amongst broken trees and branches and swamps, until I began to think it was time to return.

But by this time the sun had set, and I could not see even the glow of twilight amongst the thick trees; and I had left the river some distance behind me, and could not see that the trees were any thinner in one part than another. However I had some notion of the general direction in which I had come, and determined to turn round at once and keep towards my right hand till I came upon the river again. After going some distance I saw the swamp through which I had first past, and could trace the footmarks for some distance, and thus see what had been my previous path. I soon began to see more light through the trees, and was pleased to find myself on the bank of the river. I thought now I was out of danger, and should have nothing to do but to continue in my present course, until I came to the tent. It never occurred to me, that I might be within a hundred yards of it, and yet neither see it, nor any smoke from the fire; and that the only way in which I should be certain to find it, would be to keep upon the edge of the river all the way; but as this was broken and difficult to walk upon, and steep, I kept at a little distance from it in the wood. I walked on shooting occasionally at any birds which I saw, and it seemed as though the distance back was much greater than what I fancied I had come; but being interested in the sport and feeling quite safe, from having seen the river, I did not think much about it, but every now and then took a view of it, to be sure I was right.

At length I began to think that I remembered having seen something very much like the bank along which I was now walking, and yet I had not kept near the river in going from the tent; and I began to fear that I must have lost myself; but whether I had passed the tent, or had not yet come to it, I could not tell. However my doubt was soon ended, for in a short time I saw a high point of land which divided two rivers, and the one upon which I came was running towards my *right* hand. I was certain therefore that it was not the river upon which we had encamped; for that was running towards my left hand. There was therefore no alternative but again to turn round, and try to find the spot where my companions were. I knew that we had not gone very far before we encamped, and this time I took the precaution of keeping close upon the water's edge, without minding the soft muddy bank upon which I had to walk.

It was now late; the sun had been set some time; and it was becoming dark. When I had advanced a short distance, I saw with great delight footmarks in the mud, which were directed in the same way that I was going. I felt sure they could not have been formed by anybody but one of our own men; for ours was the only boat going up the river, and if they had been formed by somebody coming down, they would have been in the opposite direction. I soon lost them, in consequence of the ground being harder, but in a little time it became soft and I again saw them. I now began running and fired my gun; and was delighted to hear a report in reply. I ran on but could see nothing, in consequence of the many turns in the river, so I stopped, loaded, and fired again; but this time there was no reply. I hastened on, reloaded and again fired; and now the sound of the answering gun, assured me that though I could not see them I was not far from my companions. In a few minutes I heard their shouts, and on turning round a point of land, saw the boat lying in the river below, and the men sitting or standing round a bright fire which blazed upon the top of the bank. They were very glad to see me back again, for they had felt sure from the direction of the sound as I had fired in passing the tent that I had overshot the place and lost my way. If we had been twenty miles up the river instead of two, it is probable that I should not have found them. I should not have known whether I had passed them or not; and should have feared to turn back on speculation in the increasing darkness of the night. There would then have been no alternative, but to have lighted a fire, cooked what I had shot, and gone to sleep. In the morning I must have made a raft of trees and brush-wood, and floated down the river to York again. There would have been little danger in this; for the weather was not cold, so that even if constantly wet through I should have taken no harm; and I should no doubt have shot sufficient on the way down to have supplied me with food for the day or two which it would have occupied. However I was very glad to be safely with my friends again, and did not after this venture into the woods out of sight of the river.

The compass by which an Indian guides himself through the woods, when he cannot see the sun, so as to know which is north or south, is the moss which grows upon the trees. This grows best in damp shady places. Now the sun shines upon the south side of the trees, and soon dries the bark after rain, but the north side does not enjoy this advantage; consequently it remains wet, and the moss accumulates upon it. He therefore looks for the side upon which this is most abundant, and knows that when he is facing it he is looking south, and he can thus shape his course in the direction in which he wishes to go.

Two days after this, we came to the first "Portage" in the river, which term is, I believe, peculiar to this region of the world, and is derived from the French "porter," to carry—it means a part of the river where the water is so shallow, or the fall so great, that the boat can neither be rowed, nor even hauled up whilst the goods are in it. It is therefore brought to the bank, and all the things are taken out and carried by the men till they reach a place where they can manage the boat again.

The one to which we came is called the Rock Portage, from a large rock in the middle of the stream the greater part of which is out of the water. The river flows over one part of it, in a stream a few inches deep, whilst on the opposite side, it pours over it almost perpendicularly in a fall a yard and a half or two yards high. As it would be impossible to row the boat up it, it was brought close to the edge of the dry portion of the rock. The goods were all taken out and carried to the other side, and then came the most difficult part, which was carrying the boat itself. We all jumped into the water, and some taking hold of the sides, some of the seats, and some putting their shoulders under the boat, we gradually lifted it out of the water, and dragged it over the rock until we got it to the other side, at the top of the fall. Here the water was deep and we launched it again; and pursued our course.

Whilst the men were carrying the goods across, Mr. —— and I were fishing in the deep pool at the bottom of the fall. Our rod was of the simplest kind. An undressed poplar stick, ten or twelve feet long, with a piece of common string tied to the end, and having a large rusty hook, baited with a piece of trout. In a few minutes we caught a trout about two pounds weight; and in less than a quarter of an hour, another which could not have weighed less than eight or ten pounds, but unfortunately the string broke, and we could not land him. The fishes here are very large. There is a speckled fish, exactly similar to our trout, which often weighs twenty or thirty and sometimes even forty pounds. Their largest fish is the sturgeon, which is singularly shaped, seeming as if half of it were head. It oftens weighs sixty pounds, and is generally taken by spearing. Some of the Indians will not eat it, in consequence of a curious superstition amongst them, illustrated in the following story, which may be interesting as one of their national traditions.

" Once upon a time, (so an Indian story always begins,) a young Indian wished for a wife, as he had become a great hunter, and he fixed upon a beautiful young woman. His mother desired him not to choose her, but to look for a clever wife, who could dress his skins and cook well, rather than for a pretty one. But he was obstinate and persisted in his choice. In the course of two or three years they had two little boys, and lived together very comfortably.

" Some time after this he observed that his wife was always smartly dressed in the morning, and had her hair tied up, and her face painted, but in the evening, when he came home from hunting, her hair was loose, and she looked dirty and untidy. He took no notice of this at first, but as it continued to be the case, he thought it strange and fancied there must be something wrong. So one day he went a long way from home before shooting anything, and then killed a moose deer, and hung up its skin in the trees, and when he returned home he told his wife she must go and fetch the skin and meat the next day. He had never sent her for the meat before, but she durst not disobey, as this is part of the regular duty of the women, according to the custom of the country. After she had gone in the morning, he set off down the path by which she used to fetch the fire-wood, and saw another path lead from it, along which he went until he came to a place, where he saw that people had been sitting down. Whilst he waited there a young man came who expected to have met his wife,— and he now saw what had been amiss, and after fighting for some time he killed the young man. On his return home he did not say anything to his wife at first, but after supper he told her that he had killed her lover, and then he cut off her head.

"The boys had grown up to be a good size, and he knew that his rest was now at an end, for he said, 'Perhaps her gods will help her, or her brothers will avenge her.' He therefore told them that they must run away in one direction whilst he took another, and he gave them a whetstone, a knife and flint, and ten awls, such as are used by the Indians for sewing together the pieces of bark in making their canoes. They were formerly made of bones sharpened to a point, but are now always obtained from England, and are made of steel. He said to them, 'Now boys, you must run away as fast as you can, for there will be no more peace for us; your mother's body will follow me, and her head will follow you, and when it comes near you will call out, "Stop, boys, I want to kiss you!" but you must not pay any attention to it, and when it is ready to overtake you, throw one of these awls behind you, and pin it by the jaw to the ground.' So they set off, and ran as fast as they could, and after a while heard a voice calling out 'Stop, boys, I want to kiss you!' They durst not turn round to look at it, but when it came very near them the eldest boy threw an awl behind him, which struck the jaw and fastened it to the ground. After a short time the head worked itself off the awl, and followed them again, calling out as before.

"They fastened it ten times with the ten awls, and it still kept gaining upon them. When they had thrown all the awls, they did not know what to do, but the elder lad threw the whetstone behind him, and it became a high, straight rock, which stopped the head for four days; but at length it rolled itself over. They had gone a long way during this time, but at length it came up with them and called out again, 'Stop, boys, I want to kiss you!' They then struck a light with the knife and flint, and set fire to the grass between them, which stopped the head again. They ran on till they came to a river, and the youngest boy now began to cry, for he was tired, and they had no rest from the head. But they saw a crane in the river who said to them, 'Well, boys, do you want to cross the river?' They replied, that they would be much obliged if he would put them over. So he took them between his wings, and carried them across. And they told him that they were running away from the head which wanted to kill them, and begged he would not carry it over. He promised that he would not, and desired them to lie in the wood to see what would happen.

"In a very short time the head came rolling down to the bank of the river, and called the crane to carry it over. So he took it up, and when he was half way across he turned over to one side, and the head fell into the river. And immediately there came up a large sturgeon, for it was changed into one, which is the reason why some Indians will not eat this fish. Then they went on till they came to a fine lake, in which was plenty of fish; and here they remained till they became young men.

"And once upon a time as they were playing at ball upon the bank, an old conjuror came up to them in a stone canoe. He was a bad old man, and called to them to come into it. But the eldest said, 'No: they did not want to have anything to do with him.' The youngest wished to go; but when his brother spoke thus, he said no more about it. However, the conjuror by his power made the ball fall into his canoe, and the younger ran after it; and as he reached over to get it out, the old man just struck the water, and away went the canoe, for he was too great a man to paddle in the usual way, but he just struck the water, and off it went by itself. The elder was very sorry when his brother was gone in this way, and going into the woods began to cry like a wolf, for he was changed into one.

"The conjuror took the young man to his lodge, (tent, or wigwam,) and of course gave him his daughter to be his wife, for this is the universal custom of the country. He did not intend any good to the young man; and his daughter told him to get away as soon as he could, and take her with him, for her father wished to do him harm. But he said, 'Oh! no. I have fasted my share, and said prayers to many gods, and have had many wonderful dreams.'

"One day the old man said, 'I know some rocky islands in this lake, where we shall find thousands of gulls' eggs. Let us go and get some.' So they went in the stone canoe, and he told the young man to go and bring the eggs in the lap of his capôt; for he was too proud to get any himself. When he had half-filled the canoe, the conjuror struck the water, and off it started; and he called out, 'Now, gulls, come and eat him up.' Upon which, thousands of gulls immediately came, and began to peck him here and there. But the young man said, 'Oh! you little gulls, it was not in this way I dreamt you would serve me.' And then one old gull replied, 'Oh! is that you? I remember you now: How can we help you?' So he told them to come all together, and take him upon their backs, and fly with him to his lodge, which they did, and he arrived there before the old man. When he returned home he was very much surprised to see him, and said he was very sorry that the canoe started off and left him in that way. But he replied, 'Oh! no matter; no matter;' for an Indian does not profess to be offended, unless he has an opportunity of revenging himself, and intends doing so.

"In the fall of the year the old man said, 'When I was young, I used to kill moose-deer with my tomahawk. Let us go and see if we can kill some now.' So they set off in the snow, and killed three or four. And when they had made a good fire, they took off their mocassins, and leggings, and stockings, and hung them up to dry; and then cooked their supper. The young man thought something wrong was intended; so when the old conjuror had gone to sleep, he looked round and saw his shoes hanging up, and thought—'Ah! now, perhaps, he intends to burn them; and then I must walk home in the snow and get frozen.' So he got up and put the old man's shoes and stockings where his were, and put his where the old man's had been, and then went to sleep. When the old man awoke, and saw him asleep, he got up and threw the shoes and stockings into the fire, and then lay down again. And in the morning he called his son-in-law, and told him to mend the fire; when the young man exclaimed—'Oh! my shoes are burnt.' And the old man said—'Ah! you should not have gone to sleep so soon; they have fallen into the fire.' But then the young man began to examine what were left, and said—'These are my shoes, and it is yours that are burnt.' And then the old conjuror saw that it was so, and said—'What shall I do to get home?' So the young man dragged him home in one of the moose-deer skins.

"Some time after this the old man said—'Let us go out fishing.' So they set off; and when the young man was standing upon the gunwale of the canoe, he gave him a push, and cried out—'Now, serpents, come and eat him.' And two great serpents, sixty feet long, came swimming up, and trying which could reach him first. But he said—'Oh! you serpents, I dreamt of you, and you promised to help me.' Then they remembered him, and said—'Oh! is that you? What shall we do for you?' So he told them to take him back to the bank of the lake, near the lodge. And one of them looked up and said they durst not, for he saw the thunder getting up, and it would shoot them if they went near the land. (The Indians think that the thunder is a large bird, and that the lightning is its arrows, which it darts at the serpents, upon which it feeds. There is a rock in Lake Superior, called Thunder Rock, because they think that the young thunders are hatched there.) But he said that he had often dreamt of the thunder, in his fasting days, and that they were on very good terms; and he promised to pray to it not to hurt them. They then agreed to take him on shore; but he did not like them at all, for he remembered that they did not come at his call to help him, but were sent to kill him. So as soon as they got to land, he prayed the thunder to shoot them, which it did, and killed them. And he reached home again before his father, who on his return was very sorry to see the young man, but pretended to be very sorry for his accident. But he said, as before—'Oh! no matter.'

"And in the spring the old man said—'Now is the time to get some birch-bark for making a canoe; let us go and get some.' He did not want a birch canoe, for he always used his stone one; but he intended to kill the young man. So they went out; and the old man said—'We must make a support, so that the tree may not fall to the ground, or we cannot separate the bark.' And just as the tree was falling he gave it a push, intending to make it fall upon the young man; but he slipped, and it fell upon himself, and killed him. Then the young man went home to his lodge, and told his wife how her father was killed; and they lived very happily together."

In the spring, when the sap is rising, the birch-bark is easily separated from the wood, and is then used for making canoes. The bark is laid upon the ground, and cut into such a shape, that when the edges are sewn together, the canoe is made. The form is given to the canoe by means of thin ribs of birch-wood, stretched from side to side; and the seams are made watertight by pitch or birch-

G 3

gum. A canoe is thus finished in two or three days, sometimes in a single day, and is worth from 15*s.* to 2*l.*, or more, according to the size.

When an Indian wants a wife, he very seldom has anything to do in the choice. His mother arranges with somebody who has a daughter to spare, and he takes her, even if he has never seen her previously. They seldom care anything about beauty, but seek a person who can dress the skins, and make herself useful. A woman is looked upon merely as a drudge, and is, in fact, treated worse than a dog. It is not uncommon for an Indian woman, when she bears "only a good-for-nothing girl," to dash its brains out, to save it from the miserable life which she herself has led. The man does nothing but hunt and fight; his wife is expected to fetch the game home; dress and clean the skins; cut and carry home all the fire-wood; and do everything but hunt and go to battle. Many of them are also able to make very good snares for killing game.

The Indians often have three or four wives, and perhaps all these are sisters. If a man has several daughters, he looks round to see who is a fortunate hunter, and says to him—"You are a great hunter; you have only one wife; you could keep two or three. I have a daughter, will you take her?" He considers a short time, and says —"Yes." And perhaps after this, he takes all her sisters, if she has any left. There are three general methods of courtship amongst these people. The first is the most common; but the second, which has been introduced since they have had intercourse with the English, is the most approved.

The third is considered the least desirable mode, and is only adopted when a young man has no mother to arrange matters for him.

A young man's mother thinks it time he was married, as she has no inclination to continue dressing the skins of his game, as well as those of his father's. She does not consult him on the subject, but goes to some old wife who has an unmarried daughter, and takes a present of two or three buffalo's hides, and asks for her daughter. The old woman consents, subject to her husband's approbation; and announces the result the next day. The lad's mother goes back with her, and the girl packs up a few skins, or whatever she may possess, puts the bundle under her arm, and returns with her to her new home. She is told to sit down upon the son's buffalo-robe and blanket, (in other words, upon his bed,) as he is out hunting. On his return, as he enters the lodge-door, he sees a stranger-girl sitting upon his bed, and stands still or starts back. "Come in, you ragamuffin," says his mother. "The girl is too good for you; don't pretend to be too good for her." He complies.

According to the second plan, the mother is still the principal agent, and consults her son no more than in the first. She procures an eight gallon keg of rum, and invites her neighbours to "a small tea-party," and sets before them a small keg, which is soon emptied; and rum being then scarce is in request. She takes the large keg to the mother of the girl upon whom she has fixed, and offers it to her in exchange. It is accepted; the woman takes the rum to the party, they become cheerful, the marriage is considered to be concluded, and the quondam boy is now dubbed man. Some old man in the party, in the hope of getting another glass of spirit, begins an oration. He tells him that he is now a man; that he must be kind to his wife; that he will be the father of a large family, and a great man; and he pronounces a number of blessings, which multiply exceedingly with each glass of grog supplied to him in return for his good wishes.

If a boy is an orphan, and has no mother to take the trouble off his hands, he becomes acquainted with some girl whom he fancies, and if they like each other, they appear together in some place where they will be seen in public. This is the avowal of their intentions; they are now considered man and wife, and unfaithfulness is exceedingly rare among them.

But to return from this digression. We had just passed the rock portage. In the course of the day we came in sight of what is termed *par eminence*, "The Hill," from which the river takes its name. I do not know whether it has been measured, but it appears to be about 500 or 600 feet high, and is the highest ground within a diameter of several hundred miles, and from its summit can be seen fifteen or sixteen small lakes, in various directions. It is partially covered with the remains of burnt trees, which look like a number of naked poles, and continues in sight for four days, during the journey up the river. This is not entirely owing to its own elevation, but partly also to the slow progress which is made in ascending this part of the river. The rapids here are so numerous that there are often five or six portages in one day; which cause much delay. The manner of carrying the goods is simple. Each man is provided with a leathern strap, about three inches broad, which he has hitherto used in tracking, but now he employs it as a portage strap. He ties the loose narrow ends round the package which he has to carry, leaving the broad part so far from it, that he can slip his head in between it and the burden. The strap then presses against his forehead, and the load rests upon his shoulders. Another person then puts a second package on the top of this, and he starts off at a trot, which he continues till he reaches the other side of the portage, where he throws them down upon the ground. The weight which he carries each time, is about 200 pounds. Some of our men, being unaccustomed to it, did not place the strap in front of their forehead, but against their chests. They, however, soon changed their plan; for the weight of the load makes it sink down, and the strap gradually slipped up, and nearly choked one or two of them.

We came one day to a portage about a quarter of a mile long, and whilst the men were carrying the things, I thought it seemed a shame to be doing nothing. As some of our new hands did not manage very well, or appear to enjoy the work, I thought I would show them how it should be done. The path lay through the wood on the bank, and cut off a considerable point round which the river ran. Several of the trees and bushes had been cut down, so as to make a rough path; and here and there a few of the trunks had been laid down across it, forming a kind of wood pavement. In many parts, however, there were short stumps remaining, and broken brushwood sticking up a few inches above the grass and heathy moss. I had no shoes on, for it was so uncomfortable putting on wet ones, and they had become so hard and cracked from the clay of the banks during the first day or two, that I had thrown them overboard into the river, and did not happen to have put on a pair of Indian shoes before leaving the boat. I got one of the men to put my own bedding, and that of my friend, upon my head, and set off in good spirits.

I soon found, however, that it was not very easy to keep the two bundles balanced upon each other; for being tied up in the oil-cloth, they slipped with each step which I took. I had advanced about halfway across the portage, and met two or three of those whom I thought most idle, and had looked at them as much as to say, "Ah! this is the way to work," when, unfortunately for my pride, I thought too much about the example, and too little about the road; and suddenly setting my foot firmly upon the broken stem of a willow, which stood in the way, I fell down, and my burden shared the same fate. As it happened, nobody was at hand to laugh at me, so I finished the distance without having been observed.

On another occasion, I had a very narrow escape from a much more serious danger. We expected every day to meet some boats coming down the river, with one of which I was to return, but they did not know that we were ascending. I was walking alone on the bank, some distance ahead of the boat, having been led on in pursuit of some wild geese, and had on my usual clothes, viz:—a dark blue coat, and blue trowsers, and a dark blue cap, with my gun over my shoulder. Just as I turned a point of land, I saw three boats coming down the river, and not suspecting any harm, proceeded on the way. They also saw me, but not expecting to meet any one, and not seeing the boat, which was hid by the bank, they did not imagine it to be a man, my clothes at that distance resembling the colour of a black bear; and the gun they mistook for a cub. It is the custom of the black bear, when she sees any one coming towards her, to rear up, and if a cub is with her, to throw it over her shoulder, and so escape upon her hind legs into the wood. They had seen, and given chace to two bears in their journey, and were, accordingly, on the alert for more sport. Fortunately they had no rifle on board, and therefore waited till they had approached within musket shot, by which time they discovered their mistake.

The time when the black bear is in season, is early in the spring, before the snow has disappeared. When the winter approaches, he looks out for some place where he will be quiet and comfortable, and then scratches the leaves and small twigs from some neighbouring trees, and makes a very comfortable bed near its foot; he lies down, and the snow falls—it soon covers him, and forms a little mound, which is increased by drifting snow during the winter. He always keeps a small hole through this, over his nose, by means of his breathing, and this looks like a dark spot in the snow. The Indians then look for some tree which has had the branches and bark scraped from one side, and near this they find a white hillock—they look about this until they see the dark spot, and know that the bear's head is not far distant; then thrusting the handle of their hatchet through the snow till they find its exact position, they clear it away until they can give him a most unceremonious blow, just above the root of the nose, which is almost the only part in which a bear is capable of being hurt. Sometimes, however, this is not so easily managed; he lies occasionally with his fore paws crossed in front of his head, and these take off the effect of the blow; which instead of killing him, only traps his toes. Besides this, there is another inconvenience; when his paws are raised in this way, he can easily lay them upon the edge of the snow, and so drag himself out, and perhaps give chase to his pursuers. If they succeed in killing him, the skin is now in its best condition; he is very fat, and his paw is considered quite a delicacy. The Indians say that he lies one half the winter on one side, licking the paw which is uppermost, and then turns over and licks the other for the remainder of the season. Whether this be so or not, his feet are very tender when he comes out in the spring, which he does as soon as the snow begins to melt; indeed, they are so tender that they bleed freely, from walking on the sharp pieces of ice, or still unmelted snow, by which means the hunters easily track him. He is very fat towards the end of autumn, and is still in good condition on his reappearance in the world, but becomes very thin during the spring, having occasional days of abstinence, and hard work, whilst seeking for the leaves and tender twigs, which have not yet burst forth.

The black bear does not in general attack men, if he is not molested ; and even then, commonly attempts to escape. But there is another kind, which is found further to the north, called the grizzly bear, which is exceedingly ferocious. Even the boldest hunters are not ashamed to confess that they are afraid of him. They never wait for his attack, if they have time to avoid it, but at once climb up into a tree. Here they are safe, for he is the only kind of bear which cannot climb, and this is the only way in which they can escape. A gentleman with whom I was well acquainted, told me of an accident from one of these bears, which happened when he was young. Four boys had gone out with an Indian, from one of the forts, to hunt for game. They saw a bush in which were several partridges, and their guns were all loaded with shot, as they did not expect to meet anything but small game. They fired at the bush, when a large grizzly bear rushed out, which had been concealed behind it. The Indian was the nearest, and was immediately attacked, and thrown down. He knew that if left to the bear he must certainly be killed, and called out to them to fire, without minding whether they hit him or the animal. It required some time to discharge and re-load with ball, when they fired, and providentially killed the bear, but not before he had torn much of the flesh from the man's face, and almost stripped the whole from his leg

H

and thigh. The poor man ultimately recovered, and still lives, horribly mutilated and disfigured.

We were wind-bound one day during our journey, and I amused myself with arranging and pressing the few flowers which I had gathered upon the banks. It was too late in the season to find many, and the seeds of those which had faded were not yet ripe. There appear to be very few at any time, in the part through which I travelled. I found a white Anemone, similar to the one which grows in our woods; and the beautiful Grass of Parnassus, which flourishes here in great abundance. But what made some parts look very gay, was the abundance of Epilobiums, or Willow Herbs; most of which were much larger and finer than the species growing in England. Unfortunately I could not find any ripe seed, so as to be able to raise them at home. The woods are full of the Bearberry, and the Cranberry, which grows in such abundance, that in some parts you cannot walk without staining your clothes with its juice. They were just coming into fruit at this time, and the white berries formed a pretty contrast with the almost universal green around. Several kinds of gooseberries, raspberries, black and red currants, and strawberries, grow wild in the woods. They are all very small, and the currants have a bitter taste. We used to enjoy gathering them, and eating them as we walked along the banks, but we should not have thought them good, had we not been thirsty and tired. The cranberries ripen before the winter sets in, but are not gathered until the next spring, as they are much improved by being covered with snow and frozen for a few months. One of the prettiest objects in the woods was the elegant Cornus or Dog-wood, with its red bark and white berries. The Indians have a curious tradition about the colour of its bark.

"Once upon a time, Anínna Boojoð, who is their great god, and was a very famous hunter, had been out hunting, and came to a place where was an immense number of various kinds of birds, lunes, geese, ducks, and plovers, and he thought he would catch some; so he called them, and said, 'Come boys, and I will make a fire, and you shall dance, and I will play on the drum for you.' They said they would, and he made an immense fire upon the sand, and then made a drum; and said, 'Now boys, shut your eyes, and don't look, and I will play, and you must make as much noise as you can.' They all shut their eyes, and began to make a great noise; and when he beat upon the drum, they all danced in a ring round and round the fire. Then, when any fine bird came up with him, he put out his hand and caught it, screwed off its head, and put it on the ground again. After their heads are off they flap their wings for some time, and as they made a great noise in this way, the others did not know that anything had been done to them; so Anínna Boojoð continued beating his drum, and saying, 'Make as much noise as you can, boys,' until he had killed many hundreds of them.

"At last one old lune thought there was a tremendous noise of flapping of wings, and opened his eyes to see what was the cause; and then he saw what Anínna Boojoð had been doing, and he cried out, 'Oh! boys, its Anínna Boojoð;

and he has killed—oh!—hundreds of us.' Then they all began to fly away, and Anínna Boojoò was very angry with this lune, and cried out, 'Oh! you rascally lune; why did you open your eyes?' and as he had not his arrows with him, he took up his drum stick, threw it at him, and struck him upon the back, just above the tail; which made him almost come to the ground, and he had to fly a long way before he could get up again. The Lune is a large bird, and is sometimes called 'The Great Northern Diver.' There is a black spot in the feathers, in the situation where the drum stick is said to have struck him, and when taking wing, it always makes a long, horizontal flight, before it can rise in the air, both which peculiarities are thus accounted for.

"Well, Anínna Boojoò had killed many hundred birds, and said, 'I'll cook these now, and eat them some other time;' so he plucked off the feathers, and made a deep trench all round and under the fire, and put them in, with nothing but the feet sticking out, and covered them over with the hot sand; then he lay down by the fire, and fell asleep till they were cooked, having first desired his toes to look out, and awake him if the Indians came. They soon awoke him, and said 'Master, master, the Indians are coming.' He got up, and looked round and said, 'What do you mean by awaking me, and telling me so, when they are not here?' and he lay down to sleep again. The toes soon awoke him again, and told him the Indians were coming; and he looked round and said, 'What do you mean by waking me, and telling me the Indians are coming, when they are not here? I'll punish you if you do so again,'—so he again lay down, and went to sleep.

"When the Indians saw that he was asleep, they came and pulled up all his geese and ducks; plucked off the legs, and put them into the sand again; and then went away, taking all his birds with them. When he awoke he looked at his fire, and saw the feet sticking in the sand, and said, 'Oh! they are all right. I'll just see if they are cooked enough.' So he took hold of one of the legs: it came up, and he said, 'Oh! yes, they are cooked enough.' So he ate all the legs and feet, and left the rest for another time; and, when he awoke again, he began to dig in the sand, and oh! then he found that all his birds had been stolen. He was very angry with his toes, and said 'I'll punish you for this;—why did you not awake me?' So he went and stood by the fire, and held them in it until they were burned; and then he went into the wood, and some of the blood from his toes fell upon a dog-wood tree; and the bark has been red ever since."

Some of the rapids are not so high as to make it necessary to carry the goods overland, and track the boat, but they may be passed by means of poleing. Each man in the boat is provided with a long pole, which they strike upon the bottom of the river, and thrusting against them, force the boat upwards. This is very hard work in a strong rapid, and the poles are often lost, by sticking fast in a hole between two rocks or stones in the bed of the river, from which they cannot be withdrawn. It is an awkward accident if a good hand loses his pole; for, the stream is frequently so strong, that the intermission of a single stroke will allow the boat to be carried down to the bottom again.

One afternoon we had reached the top of a rapid with great labour, and the men had taken to their oars, as the water was deep again ; when, by some means, we lost ground very slightly, and, in less than a minute, were hurried rapidly to the bottom again. Almost immediately below this, the river fell over a rock of some height ; and, if we had been carried over this, going broadside on, we should, in all probability, have been drowned. Fortunately we checked our downward progress before reaching this place, and regained our former position with the same labour which it had previously cost us. It is only by seeing the force which is required to overcome the current, that we can well judge of it. One afternoon, the whole crew of thirteen were hauling the empty boat by the rope, for several minutes, without being able to make it advance in the least.

The last night of my journey up the river we encamped upon a rock, and here we had the softest bed we had hitherto found. Several young spruce firs were growing near, and we cut them down to supply the fire, and lopped off the small tufts of green leaves. These we spread upon the rock, and laying our blankets upon them, had a luxurious bed. For some time before setting off my bed had been a buffalo robe, laid upon solid boards, and, by this time I was so much accustomed to lying hard, that on my return to England, I found it difficult at first to sleep upon a common mattrass, whilst a bed was quite disagreeable.

The next morning we started early, and before breakfast met the boat coming down the river, by which I was to return. Had I gone a little further, I should have come to a small island in Knee Lake, which, as I was informed, has a remarkable influence upon the compass. It is a very small rocky island, which has not a surface, above water, of more than fifteen or twenty feet square; but in rowing round it, the compass always points to its centre, as though it consisted of a mass of magnetic ore. I believe it has never been carefully examined, to ascertain what is its nature.

CHAPTER IV.

THE journey down the river was very different from the ascent: for now the rapids which had given us so much trouble, were, if anything, in our favour. A rapid or fall, which had taken us half an hour or more to ascend, was passed in a few minutes; and, in each day's work, we saw several places where we had previously remained for the night. The comparative ease of the different directions, may be best estimated by the fact, that we came down in little more than two days, a distance which it had required eleven days to ascend.

There is something very exciting in shooting a long rapid or a fall. In general the current carries the boat down; and the men have nothing to do but to lie by their oars, ready to strike out at the slightest notice from the steersman. It is absolutely necessary that he should know every stone and rock in the river's bed, for almost every thing depends upon him. The current sometimes changes its course two or three times in a single rapid; and, frequently, there is a large stone or rock at the bottom, which would certainly stave in the boat, should it strike upon it. He therefore stands by his long sweep, and with one or two rapid strokes turns the boat's head, so as to avoid anything of this sort. As soon as it reaches the bottom he gives the signal to the men, who instantly pull at their oars,

by Google

P. 81.

to carry her out of the force of the current into smooth water, and to prevent her being overwhelmed in the eddy at the foot of the rapid.

The bowsman stands in the bow of the boat, with his long iron-shod pole, ready to push her head from any rock which may be above the water, and which the steersman, alone, might not be able entirely to avoid. He is also looking out sharply, to see if there are any hidden rocks, of which he judges by the whirling of the water above them.

There is even more excitement, and danger in "shooting a fall," than in "running a rapid." When the guides or steersmen grow old, they are often afraid of taking the loaded boat down a fall; and several times during the journey, our guide, after bringing us safely down, used to ascend by the bank of the river, to the top of the fall, to bring down another boat, the guide of which durst not attempt it. It does appear rather formidable at first, for it is just as if you were coming down a river which is crossed by a wear; and when you reach it, you allow the current to carry the boat over it, into the water below. The fall is not, perhaps, quite so perpendicular; but the risk is often increased by the current rushing round a piece of rock, against which you are in danger of striking. As soon as the boat has safely descended, and is out of danger, all the crew lay down their oars, and give three cheers. This they do as each boat passes the fall unhurt; which is an expression of pleasure and congratulation, not considered necessary in simply coming down a rapid.

Notwithstanding all their care the boat does occasionally strike a stone, and make a hole through its bottom. We had passed two or three rapids in safety one morning, when, just as we reached the bottom of another, we felt a slight blow, and saw the water rising through the side. We immediately pulled to the bank, and threw out all the goods as quickly as possible. As soon as it was emptied, the boat was hauled out of the water, and turned bottom upward, when we found that a plank had been split, and that there was a hole nearly a foot long. Every boat is provided with a saw, a hammer, a chisel, a few nails, and some oakum. In a few minutes the damaged plank was removed; a piece of wood was found, which, by a little chopping, was made to fill its place; it was nailed in; the seams were stuffed with oakum, which was driven tightly in by the edge of the chisel; the outside was rubbed with a little grease; and, before we had finished our breakfast, which we began to prepare as soon as we landed, the boat was in the water again, and ready for starting.

Most of the voyageurs, as the men are termed who come with the boats, are Canadians, who are admirably adapted to this kind of life. Their spirits are excellent, and scarcely ever cast down. If the work is very hard, or some rapid is unusually difficult to pass, or anything goes wrong, they grumble most heartily; but as soon as they are free from trouble they forget all about it, and never anticipate difficulties. If anything has to be done quickly—such as mending a boat, or making an oar, a pole, or a spoon,—they set about it, and get it finished, whilst another person would be considering how it should be done. This is an invaluable talent in a country, and under circumstances, where rapidity of action is important. It is true, that their work does not last long; but it is better that a man should be able to mend a boat in half an hour, in such a way that it will carry him the remainder of his journey, at the end of which he can get it thoroughly repaired, than that he should occupy so much time in doing it completely, that the river may be frozen up, or the ship have sailed for which the goods were intended.

The furs which came in the boat by which I returned, had been several months on the journey. They leave the Forts on Mackenzie River in the autumn, and come down as far as they can, before the ice sets in for the winter; and, as soon as it breaks up in the spring they are brought down to York. The distance is so great, and the difficulties of the journey so many, that they only arrived a few days before the ship sailed. It is not very uncommon for the voyageurs to be so much exhausted when they reach the fort, at the end of a long journey, that they throw themselves upon the bank as soon as they land, and sleep for twenty-four or thirty-six hours.

There is a great difference between the English, or Canadians, and the Indians in respect of strength. We came up with a boat manned by six Indians, and we had six Canadians in our crew. The people are very fond of running races on these occasions, and they pulled together for about half a mile, when we got ahead of them, and the race ceased. Their boat was rather deeper in the water than ours, and the stream having more power over it, brought them up with us soon after, whilst all the men ceased rowing, to eat some pimmikin. Our men were quite ready to pull another race, and had no appearance of being exhausted; but the Indians declined it.

An Indian will, however, surpass a Canadian or European in bearing cold and hunger. From their very early childhood they are accustomed to fast; partly from necessity, partly from some religious feeling which they have about it. The consequence is, that it is little or no hardship to an Indian to be two or three days without food. When they are quite young they begin to fast, generally twice a week during the winter months, and do not taste anything from supper time till the next supper time.

If they go to another Indian's lodge on one of their fasting days, and he offers them food, if they do not wish to keep their fast, they go out of the tent, and look at the sky. If the sun is bright, they say, "No; the sun will see us, and will not favour us in our dreams." But if it is cloudy, they say, "Oh! the sun cannot see us—and he will not know;" and they take the food. They continue this until they marry, which is generally when they are between eighteen or nineteen, and two or three and twenty, after which they think there is no use in fasting. If a young man can abstain entirely from food or drink for ten days together, he is thought a very great man, and is absolved from all further fasting. They are not encouraged or allowed to attempt this until they are fully grown, as it is supposed that they cannot bear it before this time. Sometimes the women also fast in the same way, and become "conjuring, or medicine women," and are then feared and respected, and so escape from some of the misery which they would otherwise endure. Their great object is to dream during their years of fasting, as they think that the more they dream the more fortunate they will be; and they treasure up all that they fancy during their sleep on these occasions. If they dream of deer or buffalo, they think they will meet abundance of game when hunting; if of bears and wolves, that they will either kill them or escape from them in safety. Sometimes they dream they see beautiful men, who appear not to be exactly like themselves; and this is a very fortunate subject. In such a case they make a very rude little image in wood, two or three inches long, which they put into their "medicine bag," and to which they pray. When an Indian can obtain food he eats to excess, and does not seem to think of saving anything against another day. Perhaps he may not have tasted food for two or three days, when he kills a buffalo, a deer, a beaver, or what not. He then eats until he cannot swallow any more, and lies down beside the fire. When he awakes he eats again, in the same degree, and again sleeps, or sets off on his journey. They do not suffer from this irregularity; and it is singular that Englishmen, when travelling in this country, and placed in the same precarious circumstances as regards a uniform supply of food, acquire a remarkable power of doing without for several days, and then eating to excess, without suffering from it. In the cold northern parts of this territory, animal food is generally the only kind which the people can procure. There is no corn, for it will not grow; and the seasons are so cold that vegetables are not cultivated. All their flour comes, therefore, either from England, or from some more southern region; and the difficulty of carrying it is so great, that little or none finds its way to some of the more remote forts. The regular allowance of animal food, when there is plenty, is eight pounds weight per day to each man; and this they easily eat, and would manage more if they had it. When they have only four pounds a day they consider themselves on short allowance; and two or three pounds would be approaching towards starvation.*

It must not be supposed, however, that this is the degree of starvation to which I have before alluded. That means entire absence of food. If their hunting has failed, or if the rivers have been frozen longer than usual, so as to prevent their catching fish, it is not uncommon for the Indians to be so badly off, that they eat the skins of the animals, instead of selling them. A short time since there was a fear that the beaver was becoming scarce, and an order was sent out that none should be killed for a few years. It was found, however, that this was not attended to; and at

* See Note A.

last permission was given to the Indians to kill them as usual, if they would only sell the fur to the forts, instead of burning it off for the sake of eating the skins.

The gentleman who told me about the adventure with the grizzly bear was once in a fort where they had no food. A party set off to see if they could find any. All the provision they were able to take with them consisted of some skins of parchment, in which it is usual to pack the furs, which they stewed at intervals during their journey. After some time they fell in with some Indians, who were as badly off as themselves; and they returned to the fort in about a fortnight, having had nothing else to live upon.

I have met with several persons who have been nearly, if not quite as badly off as this, which is not at all an extreme case. Whole families of Indians are every year killed by cold and hunger. Their hunting has, perhaps, failed; and after delaying from day to day, in hopes of catching something, they at length set off to the nearest fort. But it often happens that they never reach it: they become so much exhausted as to be unable to proceed, and are found, after some time, frozen to death. There is a regular scale in the comparative nutritious properties of different kinds of skins. Parchment comes first—it makes a pretty good soup; then follows beaver skin; fox skins taste rather strong; deer skins begin to be tough and indigestible; and an old shoe sole is about as nutritious as a buffalo's hide.

The dress of the Indians is rather ornamental when new, but it is generally so ragged and dirty that it does not look very picturesque. They wear trousers made of deer-skin, which come down to the ankles, and are fastened round the knee by a garter outside, which is generally ornamented with beads, and hangs down the leg. I cannot call to mind having seen an Indian's shirt, but if they do wear one, it is made of flannel, generally dyed blue. Their coat is called a capôt, and is made of undyed thick flannel, or blanket, bound round the edges with scarlet ribband, and having a hood behind, which can be pulled over the head at pleasure. The capôt is fastened round the waist with a long sash of scarlet worsted, in which is often stuck a hunting-knife. Their shoes are the moccassins which have been already described. Besides these things, they generally wear their fire-bag hanging from their side. This varies much in size; but is always large enough to receive the hand without any difficulty, and to contain flint and steel, touchwood, a pipe, tobacco, and what they call "weed;" which is the leaf of a species of arbutus, which they mix with the tobacco. They are generally smoking, but cannot manage pure tobacco. They begin smoking it mixed in order to save expense, and continue it from habit and choice. These fire-bags are often very handsomely ornamented with beads, long strings of which hang down from the bottom. The women wear leather trousers; but all that I saw wore also a gown, made something after the English fashion. Their head-dress is very simple; it consists of two pieces of cloth, about eighteen inches, or two feet long, and nine or ten inches broad, which are sewn together at one end, and down one side, and are just slipped upon the head. They are also much ornamented with bead work, or with figures worked in silk. Over the whole dress an Indian generally throws his blanket, which is an invaluable friend to him. It is a cloak by day; a blanket by night; a sail when he is crossing a lake; and when worn out for all these purposes, it is torn up, and converted into stockings.

It is not always easy at first sight to tell whether an Indian is a man or a woman, for they are small slender people, without beard or whiskers, and even the men wear their hair in long braids, hanging down by the side of their face. They have high cheek bones, and their colour is a kind of olive. Nearly all have dark eyes, and their hair is always black and straight, and never turns grey. I do not mean that it is always smooth, for the heads of some of the little children are complete mops, and look as if their hair had never been laid straight since they were born; but it does not curl. Many of the people are called half-breeds, and are the children of an Indian mother, and a British, or Canadian father. They are not so dark as the Indians, but their features are still well marked. They are said to be the most valuable race in the country, for they have the cunning, dexterity, and patience of the Indian, and add to these the strength of the European. They are fond of giving themselves fine names. Our bowsman was a half-breed, and called himself Black Thunder. Another man assumed the title of "The man that makes everybody fear him." From what I heard, I suspect he had a little mistaken his own character and powers; but many other people do this beside him.

When we encamped one night, in returning, he cut me a lobstick, or lopstick. This is a complimentary ceremony, which is performed for most strangers, the first time of their travelling up the country. A large tree is selected, and the man who cuts it takes his hatchet and climbs up, to within a few yards of the top, and cuts off all the branches which surround it, for about four or five yards, so that the tree is entirely bare for this space. He then comes down, and chops off the bark in front of the lower part of the trunk, making a flat, smooth surface, about a foot broad, in which space the stranger carves his own name, and that of the year. When this is done, he fires his gun over the tree; the guide of the party fires his; and the whole crew gives three cheers. Whenever that crew passes that tree it gives three cheers in honour of the stranger. This is their part of the compliment, which the stranger returns, by making them a present of a gallon of rum, or something of equal value, on arriving at the first fort.

Two gentlemen were travelling a short time since, and lobsticks were cut for them; but they professed tee-total principles, and could not think of encouraging intemperance, by giving rum. It did not seem to occur to them that though spirits might not be desirable, yet tea does not occasion much harm, and flannel is not without its uses. The next time they passed the place, they looked out for their monuments, but they had disappeared. They inquired, with some indignation, what had become of their lobsticks, "They were not yours; you never paid for them," was the reply: they had been cut down.

The Indians have a great desire for spirits, and used formerly to be supplied abundantly, as they would exchange their furs for them sooner than for anything else; but for many years the Hudson's Bay Company has been trying to break them from them, by diminishing the quantity sent out each year, and charging it a higher price. At some of the forts there is none at all, either for the officers or Indians, and the supply is very small at the others. This is made a subject of great complaint amongst the Indians; they say, "Can you get anything out of an empty nut if you crack it? so you cannot get rum out of the forts. When you first came among us, you promised that rum should flow as long as the waterfalls. The waterfalls are running still, but the rum has stopped." When we reached York, Black Thunder got no rum, but instead of it he had some tea, sugar, cloth, and duffel.

The Indians have become now, from long habit, very dependant upon the English for the supply of their necessaries; they have lost the use of the bow and arrow in many places, and rely entirely upon their guns, or upon snaring. But their guns, powder, and shot must come from England, and they generally use snares, which are also made there; and their fish spears and hatchets are all sent from this country. They make their own shoes and leather clothes, but their blankets they get from us. They appear to be well used; and pains are certainly taken to improve their condition, in a way that could not be accomplished, were not the country under the absolute control of a single company, as is at present the case.

The last day but one of our journey was Sunday; the boats travel as usual on this day, but I was much pleased with what occurred after supper. I had read the services to myself in the boat, but all the crew were Roman Catholics. There were four boats in company with us, and it is usual for each crew to make its own fire, and cook its supper independently of the others. The night was fine, but dark; there was no moon; and the Aurora Borealis scarcely showed itself: all the light we had was from the five fires in the wood upon different parts of the bank, round which we could see the parties sitting or standing, and laughing cheerfully over their meal after the fatigue of the day. As soon as supper was finished the men silently withdrew, and assembled round the most distant fire, and in a few minutes I heard our guide's voice saying some part of the Romish service, to which, at the proper intervals, the whole number responded in admirable time and order. I was too far from them to hear the words distinctly, but I could make out that they were French. I was surprised at this, but my companion told me that the Roman Catholic services are performed in French in all parts of Canada, in which this is the common language of the people; and I have since then had an opportunity of asking an English Clergyman, who resided there many years, and he confirmed this account. My companion told me that during his journey across the Rocky Mountains, and through the whole Indian country, he had often known the Indians retire in this way, and sing hymns before lying down for the night, which they had learnt from some missionaries who had been among them for a few years.

The next morning we expected to be at York, and, accordingly, great preparations were going on, for making ourselves clean before arriving there. In England, a person generally comes in from a journey tired and dirty, but it is very different here; during a journey of a month or six weeks, the men have, very likely, not washed themselves, or changed their linen once; but the day before arriving at the end of their labours they wash their shirt, which soon dries, and is clean and comfortable. Our breakfast time this day was a grand occasion; each man was shaving himself, and disentangling his hair, which had not been touched for weeks; then the clean shirt is brought into requisition, and they put on handsome new moccassins, and if they have it, a bright cotton neck-handkerchief. The delay of an hour at this period of the journey is of no consequence, and they come to the fort singing their boat songs, and in high spirits, after such an amount of long continued fatigue, that Col. Wigram, after travelling through this country, remarked, "If we were to work our soldiers in an equal degree, we should receive a shot from behind, in the very first engagement into which we entered."

CHAPTER V.

When we reached York, I became acquainted with an intelligent pleasant man, who told me a good deal about the Indians, and who was himself chief of one of the tribes of the Chippewa Indians. His native name is Pah-tah-se-gay; but that by which he is now called is Peter Jacobs. His parents were Indians, and he was brought up just like any other Indian child, and was an expert hunter. When nearly twenty years old he became acquainted with some missionaries, and ultimately became a Christian, and has been engaged for some years as a teacher, by the Wesleyan Missionary Society. Many of his tribe are Christians, so that his change did not deprive him of his chieftaincy. Amongst many of the tribes, however, a man who becomes a Christian is much persecuted; he is considered as an enemy, and an ill-wisher to his nation, and the young people are warned not to follow his example.

The Indians seem to have generally very little notion of religion, and if they are asked about their belief in a God, and in a future state of reward or punishment, will often answer, "Oh! these are things that the old people used to talk something about, but we know nothing about them." They have an undefined belief in many inferior, and in one supreme God, to whom they do not pray directly, as they think it would be presumptuous and unacceptable; but only to the inferior gods. They have no tradition of any Son of God; nor of any particular person who has the office of a Mediator, and they have very little notion of a Devil. If the power is not favourable to them, he does not often hurt them. There is, however, one whom they call "Windego" or "Mandego," who is actively opposed to them, and eats men. They think that after death all go to the happy hunting ground; but those who have been bad men go to a part where game is scarce, and where they will often be short of food, as on earth; whilst those who have been good warriors and hunters, and useful men to their tribe, go to a part which is full of animals, and where they will always have as much to eat as they wish for. After a person is dead he is buried with his bow and arrows, and each member of his family throws a small piece of meat and a spoonful of soup into the fire for twelve months; as they think that he is supported in this way, though he cannot take solid food during his journey, which occupies about this length of time. In their burial grounds, they often plant a small tree over the grave, or thrust a stick into the ground, with a piece tied to it, making it like a cross. To this they hang small strips of cloth or coloured calico, for twelve months; but I could not learn what was the origin of this custom, or what meaning they attach to it.

They seem to fancy that young children cannot find their way thither, and an affecting circumstance occurred a few years since, which illustrates this. The young son of an Indian died, and some time after his death the father said to his wife,

"Our boy cannot find his way to the happy hunting ground. Shall we go and show him it?" She consented, and he attempted to kill her; but her life was ultimately preserved. He, however, succeeded in killing himself, with this object in view.

When a person is sick, they think that he is possessed with a sick devil, and some of their conjuring or medicine men try to dispossess him: for which purpose they roll him about and knead him in every direction, in order to grasp the sick spirit in their hands, and take it away. They then retire to a fire, and open their hands over it to throw it in and burn it. If the man does not recover, they suppose that the sickness cannot be burnt, and they knead him again; but this time open their hands under water to drown it. If the man recovers they have succeeded in their attempt; if he dies, it is the sick devil which has killed him. Besides this, however, they administer certain remedies, which are few in number, but often seem to produce considerable benefit. When the sick man is first brought to the conjurors, they begin to pray in a conversational tone to their gods, and to the images which they have made, and remind them of the number of times they have appeared to them in their dreams, and how they promised to assist them when necessary: after which they proceed to their treatment.

Though want of success does not generally bring any discredit upon the conjuror, yet sometimes it is otherwise. If a relation or friend of the deceased has received any insult or injury from one of them, no matter whether he be one of those present at the time, or be at some distance, he throws out a hint that the death is perhaps owing to the evil agency of this person. This opinion is canvassed among the relations and friends, and probably rejected. He then makes a present of some trifling article to some old Indian, who repeats the suggestion, as if it came from himself. He may perhaps tempt another in the same way Its being mentioned by two or three people is generally sufficient to induce the belief, that it is the fault of the party charged; and some of the relations do not fail to take vengeance upon him sooner or later. A melancholy instance of the effects of this kind of notion occurred three or four years since. An old chief had been with some furs to the fort of which Mr. B—— was in charge, and soon after his return became sick and died; but before his death he charged his tribe to continue on good terms with Mr. B——, who had always been a good friend to the Indians. Some time after, his son, or nephew, I forget which, took up the notion that this gentleman had been the cause of his death, but it was at once discountenanced by the rest of the tribe. He however went, after several weeks, to the fort, and on arriving there was desired to sit in the place appropriated to persons coming on business, whilst food was set before him. He gave no intimation whatever of his intention, but as Mr. B—— was crossing over to the room where his wife and family were sitting, he fired at him just as he opened the door, and shot him in the back, and he fell dead in the

K

room. The young man made his escape; but, after being pursued for several weeks without success, was at length, whilst swimming across a river, shot by one of his own tribe, who all condemned his action.

When any near relation of an Indian dies, he is generally much cast down, and very seldom recovers his spirits sufficiently to hunt with energy or success for many months. It is, however, singular, that they should treat their parents as they do when they become old and infirm. If they are attacked by any neighbouring tribe, and obliged to fly from their tents, they say, "You are an old man; you are good for nothing; you cannot fight; you cannot defend yourself; you had better stay;" and they leave them; the old people themselves seldom offering any opposition. When an Indian is seriously ill, he does not often linger long, as an European does, but generally either recovers or dies quickly. This is a providential circumstance for them, as in the absence of any proper medical attendance, or any regular supply even of necessaries, their sufferings would be very great during a prolonged illness.

The conjurors, or medicine men, are a remarkable association among the Indians; and so far as they have any definite public religious services, seem to be the chief actors. They do not, however, appear in any degree to correspond with the priests of either Christian or Heathen nations. By "medicine," an Indian understands anything that is mysterious or wonderful. If he should see a person swallowing an effervescing draught, it would be "great medicine;" as would likewise the fire-eating, which is practised in playing at snap-dragon, or in eating a mince pie before the brandy is burnt out. Any animal with two heads, or six or eight legs, or monstrous in any way, is also "great medicine." The skins of such animals are preserved with great care, and put into the medicine bag. The English officers from their skill and acquaintance with many powers unknown to the Indians, are generally considered great medicine men.

The first essential preliminary to becoming a conjuror is, that the candidate shall have fasted during his youth; but this is done so much as a matter of course by all persons, that no enquiry is ever made as to where it has been practised or not. Any Indian man or woman may become a conjuror, on performing the required ceremonies, and paying the proper fees. They generally begin to pay when about eighteen or twenty years of age, and continue to do so for four years. The payments are made in skins, to the value of three or four pounds per annum, which is nearly half of what an Indian will kill in the year. His father may pay the skins for him; or if he is not able to continue his payments after having begun, he may resume them at any time. After the first year the candidate is taught some of the secrets, and more are communicated each year, until he is fully acquainted with them all. Many of their feats resemble sleight-of-hand tricks; but there are other cases in which they appear, at any rate, to possess some unknown power. They themselves believe it to be real, and imagine its origin to be evil. They think that they shall not be so happy after death as if they had not been medicine men, and that they shall be changed into animals at death ; but the authority and influence which it gives them during life, overbalances this. What their secrets are, or what power they really believe themselves to possess, Mr. Jacobs said he never could learn. On asking any conjuror who had subsequently become a Christian, the answer always was, " Those things were long ago ; we don't speak about them now ;" and he never could get any one to talk freely about them. These customs have disappeared to a considerable extent among the tribes bordering upon the white man's territory, so that Mr. Jacobs himself never became a conjuror.

There is a great festival once a year in spring, which continues about a fortnight, and is held in some good fishing station, that there may be no scarcity of food. At the commencement of this feast, the conjurors set up a large tent, the original of which seems according to a vague tradition to have been received from a set of conjurors, whose feats resembled those performed by the magicians of Pharaoh ; but they do not attach any importance to the tent itself, and if it is lost or burnt, they replace it with another.

When they are assembled in this tent, each contributes his share towards the feast. One will give sugar, another tea, a third meat, and so on. After they have eaten, the remainder is shared amongst the multitude outside, who are not, however, admitted into the tent. To this tent all those who wish to become conjurors bring their skins, and the produce is divided among those who are already medicine men. The oldest, or chief conjuror receives the largest share, and the rest in different proportions; but whatever is the age at which they become conjurors, they do not receive anything until they are about thirty years old.

One species of power said to be possessed by medicine women, rather than by medicine men, and somewhat resembling the Scotch second-sight, is that of knowing where absent people are, and what they are doing. They generally say that they feel something in their inside which tells them; but they do not possess, or will not exercise this power at all times. Sometimes when asked where a person is they will reply at once; at other times they say they have no feeling about it, and cannot give an answer. The gentleman in charge of York Factory told me a singular instance which happened in his own knowledge. A party was daily expected to arrive at the Factory, from the interior of the country, but did not come. One of these women said one day that she had a feeling in her inside, by which she knew that they were at that time wind-bound upon a certain lake, which she named, and unable to proceed, but that they would reach the Factory on a day which she mentioned. He made a memorandum of the periods fixed upon, and said, that so far as he could judge, there was nothing in the direction of the wind which could help her to guess, nor did he think it possible that she could have had any communication with Indians who might have brought the news, as the lake was distant many days' journey. On the day she named, the party arrived; and when he asked one of them where they were on such a day—"Let me see;—Oh! we were wind-bound on such a lake;" the one which she had mentioned.

The conjurors do not confine themselves simply to medicines, but also make and sell poisons, one of which is most singular in its effects. It is a light, tasteless powder, which is purchased by an Indian long before he has any particular person in view, to whom he intends giving it. One of the commonest causes of its administration, is disappointment in some love affair. He watches his opportunity, and sprinkles the powder into the kettle of soup, or upon the duck or goose, which the offending party is cooking, and being tasteless, it is swallowed unknown. No effect is produced for many months, but at length the person is suddenly seized with severe pain in the body, which continues three or four days, and then subsides; but during this time the skin has become nearly black, which colour remains through life. Mr. Jacobs tried to obtain some of the powder, but whether he was suspected, from being a Christian, he could not tell, but they would not sell him any. He has seen three or four persons, who have been thus coloured for life.*

An Indian's notions of revenge are peculiar. If any one has killed a near relation, he does not kill him in revenge, but his relation of the same degree. For instance, if a brother has been killed, he revenges himself by killing the murderer's brother. If he killed the man himself,

* See Note B.

his punishment would be immediately over, because he could not feel anything after he was dead; but if his brother is killed, he suffers the same loss and continual sorrow, which he has caused to the person injured. They do not always, however, take revenge for injuries done even to themselves. An old Indian in a fort in the interior of the country, upon Mackenzie River, lost his nose in the following way. A party had been drinking together, and having become drunk, had lain down to sleep. Whilst they were in this state one of them got up and cut off a young man's nose, with whom he had had some quarrel, and escaped. He was not aware of this immediately on awaking, but on putting his hand to his face he found it bloody, and noseless. He concluded at once that it must have been removed by the person nearest to him, who happened to be this old man, and accordingly took the opportunity of cutting off his nose, before he awoke from his drunkenness. When he found out his loss, he said, "Well, it did not matter much; he was an old man, and it was of little consequence."*

The Indians reckon the spirits of animals among their gods, and think they can hear what they say. They think they do not like to be laughed at or ridiculed, and hence they avoid doing this as much as possible. If a party of boys are talking about animals, and laughing at them, and saying what an ugly mouth an otter has, or what a clumsy, awkward foot a bear has, any old Indian who is present will stop

* See Note C.

them and tell them not to do so, for the animals will be displeased. They generally keep two or three skins of favourite animals, and put them along with the figures of the men about whom they have dreamt, into their medicine bag. They generally get young skins, and as has been already mentioned, if the animal is at all deformed, it is "great medicine." This bag is of great consequence in the eyes of an Indian; and his importance is partly estimated by its size. The chief contents are several lumps of mere clay, in addition to the skins, the images, and a very few simple medicines. If this bag is lost, as is not uncommon, by the upsetting of a canoe in crossing a river, or by a fire, the owner loses heart, and becomes quite discouraged. He loses his confidence and skill in hunting, is unsuccessful, and becomes poor, and sometimes continues in this way for a year or two. At length, at one of their festivals, he gets another bag; one friend gives him some clay balls, another a skin, and a third another skin, and thus his bag is stored, and he becomes a man again, and resumes his usual habits.

If an Indian has been unsuccessful in hunting, he thinks he has offended some of the animals. When he comes home he makes a little feast of whatever may be in the lodge, as a couple of partridges or ducks, and eats them with his family. He then goes to a corner of the tent, and hangs up his skins and figures before him, and begins praying to them, which is always done in a conversational tone, as if speaking to a friend. He commences with one, and says he does not know what he has done to offend it; perhaps he has laughed at it; he is very sorry for it, and hopes it will not think any thing of it; and then he reminds it of the number of times it appeared to him, whilst he was fasting, and of the promises it made him. And so he goes on through them all. Then he thinks he has made his peace with them; he goes the next day into the wood with confidence, and returns home successful, and fully satisfied that his prayers have been heard.

Many of these opinions are embodied in their traditions, which are handed down like our nursery tales. A number of little Indian children will give an old woman a piece of tobacco, and they will sit round while she recites them, though they may, perhaps, have heard them many times before. When the men are sitting together in a lodge, smoking, one of them will begin to relate one, to which the rest listen without making any interruption; when he has finished, another relates a second, and so on. The object of many of them is evidently to encourage adventure, and stimulate the youth to activity and skill in hunting. Their tradition about the flood is curious.

"Once upon a time Anínna Boojoò, who is the principal object of admiration and worship among the Indians, from whom they learnt to hunt, and who taught their conjurors and medicine (or mystery) men all their arts, was out in the woods seeking game. After some time he reached the borders of a lake, on the opposite side of which was a large flat rock, upon which were many red lions, basking in the sun, and observed in the midst of the herd a very fine white lion. He had often seen red lions before, but this was the first time that he had seen a white one; and he was very desirous of obtaining its skin, for the purpose of making a tobacco pouch. Now an Indian is generally contented with a musk-rat's skin for a pouch; but Anínna Boojoò was so proud, that nothing would satisfy him but the hide of this white lion. He crept through the woods with the utmost care, in order to avoid alarming the herd; but he could not succeed in coming near enough to shoot the lion; and when evening arrived they left the rock and retired into the wood, and he was very greatly disappointed.

"He would not, however, relinquish his object; but began to think how he might be more successful the next day. At length he said to himself, 'I see I shall never get that white lion's skin unless I can be upon the rock without frightening the herd;' so he determined to change himself into an old tree, and stand upon the middle of the rock, which he did before it was light in the morning. As soon as the day was hot the lions returned to bask in the sun, as before, and the white lion was amongst them. But one of the old ones, who was more cunning than the others, said, 'I do not remember that old stump of a tree upon this rock; it must be Anínna Boojoò, who has changed himself into it.' To which another replied, 'Oh, nonsense! If it is he, he cannot bear to be squeezed.' Upon which he went up to him, and squeezed him so severely, that Anínna Boojoò could scarcely refrain from crying out. 'You see I was right; it is only an old stump;' and the herd being satisfied, lay down in the sun. He then watched his opportunity, and raising his bow and arrow shot the white lion, but did not kill him; and the red lions escaping into the lake, carried their chief off with them, to his great mortification. He now began to roam through the wood in hopes of finding him, when at length he heard an old woman's voice singing and wailing most mournfully. He went to her, and addressed her, 'Well, Granny, what is the matter?'

"'Oh, my son! have you not heard what Anínna Boojoò has done?'

"'No, Granny; what has he done?'

"'He has shot our chief, the white lion; and I am going to cure him.'

"'But, Granny, what are you doing with those four strings?'

"'Oh! I am tying one to the north, and one to the south, and one to the east, and one to the west; and then, whichever way Anínna Boojoò goes, we shall catch him and kill him.'

"'And how are you going to cure the white lion?"

"'I am going to sing certain songs, and to give him what I am gathering.'

"He then learnt the songs which she was going to sing, and the direction for finding the 'lodge' in which the sick lion lay; and having done this, he killed the old woman, cut off her head, and skinned her; and then getting into the skin, and putting on her head and clothes, he went to the lodge singing the songs which she had taught him; and the lions being deceived by his appearance and feigned voice, admitted him without suspicion. He then raised his bow and arrow, and shot the lion through the heart, and killed him, and immediately took off the skin and escaped. But the lions had power to make the water of the lake rise, and it soon rose to the place on which he was standing. He went to some high ground, but the water still rose and pursued him. He climbed into a high tree, and the water continued to rise, until he was standing on its very summit, and it had reached to his chin. He began to fear that he should be drowned; when at length he perceived that the water rose no higher. But all the world was drowned, and he knew not what to do, until he saw a beaver, to which he called —'Come here, good beaver, and dive, and bring up some earth if you can, and I will make a new world, upon which you shall live, and be much happier than in the old one.' So the beaver complied; but he dived so deep and long, that he was suffocated, and rose again, dead. He then saw a sea otter, to which he made the same request; and he also complied, and with the same result. He began almost to despair, when he saw a musk-rat, (musquash,) which is a very quick and good diver; and he made the same request and promise to it. The rat dived, and was long down, and at length rose apparently dead; but Anínna Boojoǒ shook it, and rolled it in his hands, and blew upon it, and breathed into its mouth; and, after a while, it began to breathe again, and opened its eyes. Then he examined its claws with great care, and found a very small portion of earth sticking to them, which he took and rolled in the palm of his hand, frequently breathing upon it.

And as he did so it increased until it was the size of his hand; when he laid it upon the water, and drew his finger round the edge, until it was large enough to bear the rat, which he then placed upon it. This walked continually round and round, until it increased, so as to bear the weight of an otter; and so on, until it would support all large animals: and thus Annína Boojoò made the world again.

One of the islands in Lake Superior is thought by the Indians to be the commencement of this new world.

"Anínna Boojoò once caught a very fine porcupine, which is considered quite a dainty among the Indians, and having dressed and cooked it, sat down to eat it. It happened that the wind made two trees rub against each other, so as to produce a creaking noise. Anínna Boojoò was so proud that day, that he had a very delicate stomach, and could not eat if there was any noise. So he said, 'I can't eat whilst those trees are making that noise;' and he climbed up to separate them. But just then they caught one of his arms between them, and held him fast. And some Chipewa Indians looked up from the bush, and saw him, and said, 'Oh! Anínna Boojoò is fast. We'll go and steal his porcupine.' So they took it, and ate it; and he could not come down, until the wind changed, when the trees separated and set him at liberty.

"Once upon a time he saw some very little strange-looking children upon the banks of a lake, and said to them, 'Who are you?' they replied, 'We are called frighteners.' So he spit upon them

L

and laughed at them, and went and lay down by the lake. And whilst he was asleep he heard a tremendous noise close to his head, and was so startled that he rolled over into the water. It was some partridges who had made this noise, because they were offended by his insulting the children, which were young partridges.

"Once upon a time seven Indians determined to visit him, and found it would take them seven years to reach the 'Happy Hunting Ground,' where he lives. One of them was good friends with the Grizzly Bear, and was protected by it for a year, and the rest of the party for his sake. Another had dreamt of the Buffalo, and he provided them with meat, for a year; and so on with each, for the whole time. When they came to Anínna Boojoò's lodge, they saw it surrounded with buffalo, moose-deer, and beavers' bones; which were signs of great plenty. He asked the cause of their visit: and when told that they wished to become great conjurors by means of his instructions, he reproved them, and said he had long since given them to the conjurors in the east country, and they ought to be satisfied with that. He then invited them to a feast, and after they had eaten, he told them to dance. And immediately the animals began to dance round them; and then he desired them to shoot as many as they wanted, but not more, as he could at any time assemble them round him, by playing music to them. Then he inquired what they wanted: and one asked that his hair might become quite white; which meant that he might live to be so old, that his hair should change its colour, which an Indian's does very slowly, if at all. And this was granted. Another asked that he might never die: and Anínna Boojoò pointed to a stone, and said, 'Do you see that?' And he turned him into a figure of granite, and said he would never change, but would live for ever in that form. The rest were so frightened, that they only asked to become very great hunters, and medicine men; which was granted. After this, they stayed with him three months, and then left him, and became very great men when they returned home.

"Once upon a time, an Indian and his wife lived in a wood, near the nest or 'wash' of a large white bear, which came out and killed and ate them both. They had two children, a girl and a little boy. The girl was old enough to snare rabbits and small game, so that they could get what was sufficient to live upon. The bear left them, and said to himself, 'I won't kill them now, but I'll wait till they are grown up, and worth eating; and then I'll kill and eat them.' They grew up till the boy began to be able to shoot; and at length he shot deer and large animals, and became a good hunter. One day he said to his sister, 'Sister, where does this path in the wood lead to?' And she replied, 'Oh! brother, you must not go along that path; for it leads to where there is a very great white bear, which killed our father and mother; and I know he's only waiting till you are grown up, to kill you too.' 'Oh, no, sister, I'll not go along that path.' So he set off another way, and then turned round, and went to the very place against which she had warned him. And while he was looking about, he saw the great bear lying very near him, and he began to recall his dreams, and to call upon his gods, who had promised to assist him, and to tell them that they always promised he should kill whatever he saw. The bear got up, and just as it came forward, he let fly an arrow at its heart, and killed it. Then he thought himself a very great hunter, and took off its skin, and returned to his sister, and said, 'See, sister, I've killed that tremendously large white bear.'

"Once upon a time, he said to his sister again, 'Sister, where does that path in the wood lead to?' 'Oh! brother, you must not go along that path; for if you do, you will never come back again.' 'Oh, no, sister, I'll not go along that path.' So he went another way, and then turned round, and came into the same path a good way off. He went on till he reached a river, where he saw a great many birds flying about; and he shot an arrow at one, but it flew over it, and fell into the river. He did not like to lose his arrow, so he jumped into the river, singing, in defiance to all fishes, that they could not hurt him; and just as he had regained his arrow, and was swimming back, a great masquenúnja swallowed him. This name means literally 'a tremendously large fish,' and is applied to the largest kind of Jack fish. His sister was a medicine woman, and she felt something inside her, and said, 'Oh! my brother has gone to the river, and a fish has swallowed him.' So she set off to the river, and reached it that day. The next day she pulled off a great deal of the bark from the bass-wood tree, and made a rope sixty feet long; and having fastened a sharp bone to one end of it, she secured the other end to the side of the river. This took her all the day, and on the third day she began to fish with it, and prayed to her gods at the same time, that the fish which swallowed her brother might take it. After a while a large Jack fish caught it, and she could scarcely haul it in. But she continued pulling; and when she got it to shore, she cut it open, and then found her brother, who said, 'Oh! the dirty fish has dirtied me.'

"Once upon a time after this, he said to his sister, 'Sister, where does that path in the wood lead to?' She replied as before, 'Oh! my brother, you must not go down that path; for a great many people have been down it, and nobody ever came back; and you must not think yourself such a great hunter that you can manage it.' To which he returned an answer as before, and acted in the same way. After entering the path, he travelled all day, until he came at night to a place where it ended in a large open plain, in which was a deep hollow. He stopped, and said to himself, 'I never dreamt in my fasting days of going down into a pit, and my gods coming to help me; so I won't go down here; but I'll set a snare, and see what I can catch.' So he made a snare, and set it just upon the edge of the hollow; and then lighted a fire, and cooked his supper and went to sleep. In the morning when he awoke, he went to see his snare, and found something very round and shining in it, and saw that he had caught the sun by the neck as it came up in the morning. And he said, 'Oh! I have done very wrong to catch the sun, for the Indians in the west will

L 3

want him during the day; I must let him loose.' So he called to a moose-deer, 'Moose-deer, go and let the sun out of the snare.' And the deer went. But when he came near, it was so hot that he was burnt to death. Then he called to a buffalo, 'Buffalo, go and let the sun out of the snare.' And he went to let him out. But when he approached, the sun was so hot, that he was burnt to death. So he looked round and called the mammoth, and said, 'Mammoth, go and let the sun out of the snare.' And the mammoth went and loosed the sun; but it was so hot that he was burnt up all but a little piece about the size of the end of your finger, which was changed into a mouse. Then he went back to his sister, and she knew where he had been: for she had seen that the sun did not rise at the right time, and being a medicine woman, she knew that he had caught it."

There is a very small black mouse in Canada, about half the size of a common English one, which is said to have been formed in this way.

"Once upon a time, a young Indian hunter said to his sister, who was a medicine woman, 'Sister, where does that deep path in the wood lead to?'

"'Oh! my brother,' she replied, 'you must not go along that path, for many people have gone down it, but none ever return.'

"'Well, sister, but I cannot stay here all my life. I must travel, and be a man, and seek a wife. There is plenty of dried meat, to last you two or three years. Will you make me some shoes?' She at length consented, and made him a dozen or twenty pairs, and he set off.

"After travelling two or three days he came to a

village, and was conducted to the chief's tent, or 'lodge.' After supper, the chief said he was very sorry he had come, for a great giant, called Windego (or Mandego), came every morning to the village, and took away and ate two men, and had destroyed nearly all their people. But he replied, that he had had many dreams, and had never dreamt of being eaten by a giant, and was not at all afraid. So in the morning the giant came to the tent, and demanded the stranger; but the chief begged he would not insist upon it, for he was a stranger, and must be treated hospitably and sheltered. He, however, persisted in his demand; upon which the young man came out singing and praying to his gods. When Windego saw him, he was very angry, and said, 'What do you mean, boy, by coming out and making that noise? I am going to eat you.'

"'Oh! no,' replied he; 'I will kill you instead.' So he let fly an arrow which struck him in the heart and killed him. His own tomahawk was too small, so he took the giant's, and with it cut off his head.

"He then went forward to another village, where the same events happened; and this was repeated ten times. When in the last village, the chief told him he would meet no more Windegos, but would come to three lodges, a day's journey from each other; that there would be an old woman in each, who would treat him very kindly on his arrival, but would kill him during the night, if he fell asleep; so that he must on no account go to sleep, however tired he might be.

"Accordingly he arrived by night-fall at the first

lodge, and, going in, he addressed the old woman with, 'Well, Granny! what cheer?' who replied, 'Come in, my Grandson.' He then told her that he was very hungry, and she gave him some dried blackberries for his supper. There were not more than he could hold in his hand, and he thought, 'I shall never be satisfied with so little as this;' but, as he ate, the berries became more numerous, and he could not finish them. He then lay down, and pretended to go to sleep; but watched, and soon saw the old woman rise, take a tomahawk, and come towards him, upon which he jumped up, and seizing his own, he killed her.

"The third night, the old woman told him, after he had eaten his berries, that he would come to no more lodges, but would reach a river without any ford, where he would see a mud turtle that would carry him over if he gave it some tobacco. She also intended to kill him, as the others had done, but he killed her instead.

"About noon, the next day, he came to the river, and saw a large turtle, to which he said, 'Turtle, I will give you some tobacco if you will carry me over the river.'

"It agreed, and took him upon its back; but, when half over, it said, 'I have a great mind to let you sink, by swimming from under you.'

"'You had better not, for if you do I will shoot you.' It then carried him safely across.

"He soon came to an old man's lodge, who wished him to stay; but he would not. So the old man told him he would come that night to a lodge, through which the path lay, and through which he must pass, if he would continue his journey.

He added, that ten young girls lived in it; nine of whom would offer him black fruit, and try to pull him towards themselves, and invite him to stay with them; but the tenth, who was at the furthest end of the lodge, would offer him a white fruit. He must push on till he came to her, and he might stay with her in safety. He then gave him two large round stones, and twelve long sharp-pointed bones, saying, that they might, perhaps, be useful to him, and regretting that he had nothing more valuable to offer him.

"He then proceeded on his journey, and by night reached the lodge, through which he pushed his way, being in some degree assisted by each one trying to pull him from the other, so that he came at length to the tenth, who offered the white fruit, with whom he stayed. After supper he asked his companion what was the meaning of the nine girls that he had seen. She told him he was very fortunate in having passed them, for if he had not, he would have been killed that night. They were ten sisters; and the first nine were married, the husbands being all large serpents. In general, the traveller, being tired, did not care with whom he stayed, and the husband then came out and killed him. Upon this he looked and saw nine large serpents asleep in the tent, and the women asleep also. So he put the two stones into the fire, and when they were hot he choked first one and then another, until he had killed them all, by thrusting them down their throats.

"The next morning he went on his way, but could scarcely distinguish the path. Many previous travellers had come as far as this lodge, but here they had always been killed; so that the path up to this point was good, but beyond it, the untrodden grass and wild flowers left scarcely a mark to guide his steps. He, however, went on, and by night came to a steep hill, on the summit of which was a lodge. This he entered, and saw an old woman and her daughter, the former of whom he saluted as before, with, 'Well, Granny! what cheer?' She invited him in, and made him some supper; after which she said that she wished he would marry her daughter, for she had never before seen any one to whom she had liked to give her.

"In the night the daughter awoke him, and told him he must not stay, for her mother meant no good to him; and she wished he would go away and take her with him. She said her mother would pretend to be sick in the morning, but it would only be to lay some trap to do him harm. But he replied, 'Oh! I have dreamt many dreams in my fasting days, and nothing was ever to hurt me.'

"In the morning the old woman did pretend to be sick, and he said, 'Well, Granny! what's the matter with you?'

"'Oh, my son, I am sick. I want some lion's flesh. That would make me well again.'

"So he said he would try to get her some; and she showed him a ledge of rock, where were many of them, intending him to go amongst them, when they would kill him. But he went up a higher ledge and met one by itself, which he killed and took home. Another morning she again pretended to be sick, and said, 'Oh! I remember, when I was a girl, I used to ride on a carriole down such a beautiful slope; if I could have a ride now I should be quite well.' He offered to accompany her; so she got the carriole, and took him to the summit of a slope, and desired him to get in in front, and she would sit behind. When he was seated she gave the carriage a push, and sent it down the slope and right over the edge, for she had taken him to the end of the world.*

"Whilst he was falling, he prayed to his gods that he might not be much hurt; and when he came to the bottom he looked up, and saw that he had fallen from a tremendous height. However, as he had his long sharp bones with him, he thought he might climb up again; so he took two of them, and by sticking them into the side of the rock, one above the other, and pulling out first one and putting it in higher, and then the other, he got up very slowly. He wore out one pair every day, and it took him six days to get up; and just as his last pair was worn out, he could put his hand upon the top, and get upon the world again. He then went back to the lodge, and simply said, 'Ah! you old woman, you played me a nice trick.' She pretended to be very sorry, and she was very sorry to see him come back.

"At night his wife wished him very much to go back to his own home, and to take her with him. So he took her and tied her to one of his arrows, and shot her in the direction of his lodge, and she fell a few yards from the tent door. He then set

* The Indians think that the world ends abruptly in a steep hill.

off running, and his gods helped him, so that he reached home in a few minutes. And when he came to his wife he said he must go and tell his sister, before he took her to the lodge. When he got there, he saw his sister looking very dirty and neglected, and he called, saying, 'Sister, I have come home again.' But instead of looking up, she only threw ashes in his face, and said, 'Get away, you idle foxes; you have cheated me so often.' For he had been away a long time on the whole; and soon after his departure the foxes used to come and cry out, 'Sister, sister, I have come home;' so she thought it was merely they that had returned. But he went in, and then she was very glad to see him; and he brought his wife to her, and they lived very happily together all his life."

We soon took in our cargo, and returned to England. On the homeward passage we passed one or two icebergs, but that was all the ice we saw. Nothing of any interest occurred until we approached the Irish coast. We had had much contrary wind, and had not seen the sun for eight days, and, as we found afterwards, had been driven a good deal out of our reckoning.

Many people have an undefined notion, that in the expression, "And now, when neither sun nor stars, in many days appeared, all hope that we should be saved was taken away," is meant that it was dark for several days and nights. It simply means that the sky was so covered with clouds, that they could not see the sun; and, as they had no compass, they could not tell how they were steering, whether north, south, east, or west.

We had been, then, eight days without seeing the sun, and did not know exactly where we were, but believed that we were entirely south of Cape Clear, the most southerly part of Ireland. The wind had been blowing all day in such a direction, that it would have carried us directly upon the coast, had we been near it. When the first watch was set for the night, it changed, and instead of blowing upon the coast, blew down along it. It was thick and foggy at midnight; but about one in the morning the rain cleared off, and the mate upon watch saw that we were fast sailing upon the rocks, and were so near, that he fancied he could almost have leaped upon them from the deck. We were probably a mile or two distant; but had the fog continued a quarter of an hour longer, we should almost certainly have struck, and gone down to the bottom. As it was, the change in the wind allowed him to put the ship's head about, and so change her course, which he could not have done, had it remained as it was before the night-watch was set. The captain was instantly upon deck; but it was some hours before we were out of danger of being carried upon the rocks, which are here almost perpendicular, and very high.

It was the eighteenth day of the month; and we surely proved the truth of the psalm for the day—"He shall give his angels charge over thee, to keep thee in all thy ways. They shall bear thee up in their hands, that thou hurt not thy foot against a stone."

In a few days after this we reached home in safety.

M

CHAPTER VI.

The next summer I sailed again from London to Hudson's Bay, but in the Prince Albert, bound for Moose Factory, James's Bay, instead of in the Prince Rupert. We remained a few days at Stromness, as in the previous year, and sailed thence on the 26th of June, and crossed the Atlantic without meeting with anything worthy of comment. We had some contrary winds, which drove us out of our course; but when we had been at sea about a month, we calculated, from our reckoning and observations, that we were approaching the entrance of Hudson's Strait. As usual, the weather was thick, so that we could not see far a-head. At length we found that we ought to be sufficiently near Resolution Island to see it in the course of the day, unless there was some mistake in our calculation. About noon the fog became rather less dense, and we fancied that we saw in the haze the outline of the southern cape. We were preparing to telegraph our consort, the Prince Rupert, that we saw land; but wishing not to make any mistake, we waited a while longer, and continued our course. We imagined that we were now sailing along the coast of the island, and that we were ten or twelve miles distant from it. Between three and four o'clock in the afternoon, the fog cleared away for half an hour, and we saw the bold, characteristic outline of Resolution, distant eight or ten miles. Thus, after having been out of sight of land for several weeks, and having had contrary winds, which had driven us out of our course, we found that we were within half-a-dozen miles of the place where we thought ourselves to be; and were assured of the accuracy of our observations.

We had not advanced along Hudson's Strait so far as we did the last time, before we saw the Esquimaux. We were becalmed off Saddleback, which is one of the range of islands upon the north shore; and in the evening a few canoes came towards the ship. When they arrived, some of the men thought they recognised old acquaintances among them; but if so, our friends had become poor since the last voyage. They had very little ivory or whalebone, and no oil. This time the sea was smoother than before, and two canoes came off with women and children. These canoes were very different from those used by the men. They are large, square, and flat-bottomed; and will hold twenty women, besides dogs, children, and puppies. The last two, indeed, are sometimes mistaken for each other. One little juvenile narrowly escaped an untimely end. Its mother had put it in the bottom of the boat, under one of the seats, that it might be out of the way. It was wrapped up in seal and deer skin clothes, and looked like a little mound of dirt and hair. One of the sailors was getting into the boat to buy something, and wishing to put his foot there, was about to give the supposed puppy a good kick, as a notice to move, when he fortunately discovered his mistake just in time. The women row with long paddles, as we manage a boat with oars; the only difference is, that their paddle has a large round end, like a plate or trencher, which they dip into the water. An old man steers, with a similar paddle, instead of a rudder.

I cannot say much for the beauty of the women, whose faces, though cheerful and good-humoured, would have been improved by the use of soap previous to coming to the ship. Their hair is dark, like the men's, and very neatly braided at the sides of their faces, and turned up behind. Their features are strongly marked, and look coarse, from their high cheek-bones and their broad faces. The little children, however, made quite an impression on board.

Whilst they are young, their features are not nearly so decided as when they are older, and they have bright black eyes, and a pleasant hearty smile. There were two in particular with whom I carried on a brisk trade. They had brought a number of little figures carved in bone or ivory, and representing the different kinds of animals and birds which are met with in the Straits; as the walrus, or sea-horse, the seal, the white bear, and the various birds which swim upon the water. They had also little ivory figures of men and women, which were very well executed, and give an admirable notion of the style of people, and of their dress. I bought one figure of a man which had perhaps been a favourite doll with one of them. It is about a foot high, and is completely dressed in seal skin, like a real man. The different parts, as his jacket and trousers, are sewn with sinews, and would not disgrace, in their fitting, many a tailor of celebrity. The face is entirely gone, though whether it has been worn away by kisses I cannot say. The figures of the birds and animals have a hole through some part of them, and were all strung upon a piece of sinew, so as to form a necklace. I had this time provided myself with some glover's needles, which are much more valuable to these people than common round or darning needles. They are made strong, and are ground so as to have three edges which run from the point nearly to the eye, and it is much easier to sew leather with them than with round ones, which are very apt to stick, and are forced witn difficulty through the hole made by the point. For one or two of these I received two or three figures; and as the little girl consulted her mother before concluding the first bargain, and had her approbation, we were mutually pleased with the exchanges. Her stock was soon exhausted, when another little smiling beauty stretched out her hand with two or three in it. I was about to take and examine them, but she seemed afraid to part with them, before receiving their value in return. However the girl with whom I had been trading said something to her, which I did not understand, but concluded to mean, "You need not be afraid, he is quite honest;" at any rate it fully satisfied her, and she again held out her hand, and we finished the bargain very quickly.

When I had bought all they had, there were still two or three needles remaining, so I thought I would be generous, and make them a present of one each, which I accordingly offered them. This seemed to puzzle them exceedingly. They searched

M 3

their pockets, and they searched their bags, to find what it was that I wanted in exchange—and appeared as if they could not understand that any one should be so liberal as to give a needle for nothing. At length the little one found a small piece of rabbit skin, which she offered, and as I expressed much pleasure in receiving it, this set her mind quite at rest. One of the party in the other ship nearly concluded a purchase which he did not intend, and from which he was glad to draw back. He offered a good woman three needles for her infant, which were accepted, and she gave him the little hopeful. He was not quite sure whether she really meant it, and in order to try her, began to move off with it. He was, however, rather alarmed to find, that she not only was in earnest but was of the opinion expressed in Doctor Syntax's tour—

"If 'tis the same thing, sir, to you,
Make the gift double and take two."

He had not gone above a step or two before he felt her pluck his arm, and offer him another on the same terms. He did not however wish thus to increase his family, so he hastily returned his purchase, lest the boat should set off, and leave him with his little charge. They remained about the ship as usual till after midnight, when they returned to the island, and we continued our course.

We saw many more icebergs in the Straits than during the previous voyage, but not so much field ice. We counted at one time from the deck fifty icebergs, large and small, but these we could easily avoid, and as there were no large fields of miles in extent, we were very little delayed, in our passage through the Strait. We congratulated ourselves upon this, and thought how soon we should be at Moose, forgetting the old adage, about not shouting before being out of the wood. We parted from our consort off Mansfield Island; she was to go to York, whilst we were to proceed down James's Bay to Moose. It is very common to meet with ice in James's Bay, but there is not generally much in Hudson's Bay. We had not, however, sailed a hundred miles south of Mansfield, before we saw it, extending in every direction a-head of us, as far as our eyes could reach.

We wished to avoid it if possible, and accordingly sailed along its edge for two days, in hopes of being able to find some open passage through it, but in vain; as far as we could see it looked like a high wall of solid unbroken ice, which seemed to become thicker the farther we advanced. At length we saw a narrow crack, and as it lay directly across our course, we determined to enter it, in hopes of finding that it was only the outside, which was so firmly packed. We entered, but soon repented of having done so. We sailed along for a short distance, striking occasionally against heavy pieces of ice, and making but little way. After a short time it became still thicker, the ice closed behind us, and we were set completely fast. We cast anchor as usual to the largest piece which was near us, and said to each other, "Oh! it does not matter, we have plenty of time yet, it is only the 3rd of August. If we are there in a fortnight we shall do very well," and so tried to make light of it. The next day, the ice opened a little, and we set the sails and took up the anchors. We worked very hard, now turning to one side, now to another, and now going backwards, in order to avoid large pieces of ice; and when the field again closed upon us, we had sailed nearly four miles. Again we cast anchor, and again we said it was of no consequence; but this time we remained fast for two or three days. Then the ice opened a little, and for three days we managed to force our way through about two miles of ice each day; but on the fourth we made a noble stretch and sailed nearly twelve miles. Unfortunately, however, we were not much benefited by this progress; for we wished to go south, and the ice only opened towards the east, so that we did not actually gain anything.

And now one or two of those who had come out for the first time, began to have rather long faces, but did not say anything to us, though we used occasionally to hear them talking together upon deck, and expressing their hopes and fears. The last voyage the ship was fast for twelve days, though not actually frozen up, so we comforted ourselves by saying, it was no worse than it had been before. But now the twelfth day had passed, and still we were not free, and we could see no probability of this being the case. Sometimes the ice opened and all hands were busy getting the ship under weigh again—but it was only to be disappointed. We sailed perhaps a mile, then a large piece of ice lay across her bows, and she could not be got past it. All hands were then set to the long ice poles, and tried to push it away from her head, and after half an hour's hard work, this was perhaps accomplished. She would sail for a half a mile further, or often not even her own length, before she was again stopped, and this obstacle was removed only to make way for another, which would detain us for many hours.

We had now been fast for three weeks; and August was nearly gone. Everybody began to be anxious. The new hands asked, "Shall we have any chance of getting back this year, sir?" and the boatswain, who was an old hand, and a married man, said, "A dismal look-out this, sir;" and true enough it was so. From the deck, or from the mast-head, we could scarcely see as much water as would allow of the lead being thrown overboard, to find how deep it was. The married men looked dismal, and talked about their families; and the bachelors said, "See how much better off we are than you:" though I do not think even they felt entirely at their ease. We began to speculate as to the cause of our unusual detention; and many likely and unlikely reasons were assigned. To most people it would have appeared probably owing to a severe winter and a late spring, which had not been able to break up and disperse the ice; but this was not a sufficient or satisfactory reason to Jack. It was at this time that our evil deeds came to our minds, and furnished us with a much more efficient cause. In the first place, the second mate remembered, that when the ship was launched she carried away one of her cradles, or pieces of timber, upon which she had been supported; and many people remarked at the time, that it was a very queer looking thing for her to do so. Besides, it was unlucky that she had not been named after the Prince of Wales; an old ship which had made many successful voyages to these parts. This partly accounted for it; but something more weighty still remained behind. We had been in Orkney, and had shot an old woman's cock. The mate remembered a whaling ship which touched at Perth, and one of the sailors went on shore, and carried off a cock belonging to an old woman there. She came on board, and having in vain demanded payment for it, she laid a curse upon the ship, and said it should never accomplish its voyage. It sailed, and, after meeting with many difficulties, was forced to return, quite unsuccessful. Could anybody, after this, doubt why we were blocked up in the ice? It is true that it was somebody from the other ship who had shot the bird; but what had that to do with it? I had been of the party; it was my gun which was used; and we were paying the penalty.

When we had been fast about a month, we had a very heavy gale, which continued almost without intermission for six and thirty hours, and then subsided. We thought that this would surely make such a movement in the sea, that the ice would be broken up, and we should be able to get out. It did open a little, and we sailed a few miles, when it closed again; and we were again fast for three days. I took an observation of the moon one night, and found by it that we were six miles south of our position at noon. Though we had been sailing the whole afternoon, six miles seemed such a distance, that I thought there must have been an error in the observation, for it was impossible we could have gone so far in only half a day. It was, however, correct; we had actually advanced six miles in nine hours. It was long before we did so good a day's work again.

I was one day sitting reading in the cabin, when the captain called down the companion, "Doctor! Doctor! quick upon deck. We are in open water." I instantly ran up, and saw that we were indeed in open water, for it extended about a quarter of a mile a-head, and was two or three hundred yards broad. The ice, however, soon closed again; and we had no more prospect of getting out, than we had when we first entered. The ship was often so completely fixed, that even high winds did not move her. One day we had all our sails set for eighteen hours, with half a gale blowing the whole time, and we did not move a single yard. At length we took in sail, fearing that the masts would not be able to bear it.

It was very discouraging to find ourselves frequently driven back a considerable distance, after toiling hard for several days in getting towards the south. Sometimes for two or three days we moved southward through the ice, and thought that we gained some distance, but when we took an observation of the sun, we often found that we were actually further off at the end of a week than at the beginning. It seemed as if a current had carried us and the ice together towards the north, whilst the wind carried us through the ice towards the south.

During this time the weather was very cold for September, though not severe, if we thought of it as winter. In a single night the water, in the spaces between the masses of ice, was frozen a couple of inches thick; and it often happened, that the ice formed in the night was so strong, that it required a good wind to enable the ship to break it up, even when there were no large pieces in her way. One of the sailors came to me one morning, with both his cheeks frost-bitten, which was a remarkable thing to occur in the first month of autumn.

The only time of real danger was during or after a heavy gale. When this had continued several hours, it caused waves five or six feet high; and these made the heavy ice amongst which we were lying strike against the ship's sides with so much force, that if she had not been very strongly built, she must have been broken by the violence of the blows. It was fortunate for us at these times, that we were so completely beset; for if there had been greater space between us and the ice, the pieces would have struck us with much more force; as it was, they had not time to acquire much impetus before they reached us. When we had been blocked up five or six weeks, nobody pretended any longer to think that we should be able to return home; for we fully expected that if we could even force our way south before the winter came on, we should not be able to repass the ice in coming northward. We, therefore, made up our minds to spend the winter upon Charlton Island, which is in James's Bay, and prepared our hatchets for felling the trees of which to build our houses. These would have been soon erected, and we had abundance of provision on board, to last us through the winter; we also had plenty of blankets; and as the island is covered with wood, we should have had sufficient fuel to keep ourselves warm. We could not have remained in the ship, for it is necessary to take it out of the water, in order to prevent its being damaged by the ice which comes down the rivers, when they begin to break up in the spring. The highest tide is in November; we should have lightened her by taking out all the goods and the ballast, and the tide would then have carried her so high upon the beach, that she could have lain there safely until spring, when she could have been floated again at some high tide.

In building the houses, a hole is dug in the ground three or four feet deep, the size which is intended for the house. The trees are not squared, but simply have their branches lopped off, and are then laid flat one upon another, and the spaces filled up with moss, and covered over with clay or mud. No wind can then get through; and when the snow falls, it accumulates round the building, and makes a wall many feet thick. By digging the hole, a much smaller number of trees is required, and the house is much warmer than if it were entirely above ground.

Sometimes the companies of the ships have been very badly off when they have had to winter. They stayed one year at Churchill, which is to the north of York. Provisions became scarce, and a party of seven or eight men were sent to York to obtain more. They were to travel by land, and two Indians went with them as guides; it was expected that they would arrive there in about a fortnight, and provisions were given them for that length of time. The ground was covered with snow before they set off, and they took their food and blankets in sleighs, which they dragged after them. Unfortunately, there were but two pairs of snow-shoes in the party, and they therefore got on less quickly than was expected. These shoes are very necessary in walking upon the snow; they are flat, about two feet and a half long, and a foot or eighteen inches wide; square at one end, and pointed at the other. They are made of a piece of wood, which is bent into the proper shape, and forms the frame. Cross-lines are made by thongs of deer-skin, which are platted together; the foot is placed in the middle, and a narrow band is stretched across, like the band of a patten, which keeps the shoe from falling off. Being so large, it does not sink in the snow as the foot would do, and a person walks with much less fatigue, but it requires a little practice to avoid knocking the ankles, in moving the foot forward. They are very useful for another purpose. At night it is necessary to contrive some shelter from the cold: a hole, four or five feet deep, is dug in the snow, large enough to contain all the party besides their fire; a large fire is made at one end, and brushwood, or branches of trees, are spread a foot thick at the other end, to make a bed, and keep the people off the snow: they then wrap themselves up in their blankets, and lie down with their feet towards the fire, and sleep very comfortably. The snow-shoes form excellent shovels for digging this hole.

This party was a good deal puzzled one day, and rather alarmed, by some marks in the snow, which were in two lines. One was evidently formed by a common snow shoe, but the other was round, and not nearly so large; and they thought this must be the footmark of some unknown beast, which had followed the owner of the shoes. When they arrived at the end of their journey the mystery was explained :—a man was travelling, who had a wooden leg; he wore a common snow-shoe upon his own foot, but a smaller round one upon the end of his wooden companion.

They had, however, many real causes of fear before reaching their desired place. Owing to their slow progress, from the want of shoes, their provisions fell short; and at last the whole were finished. One of the party became so feeble and exhausted, that he fell down many times a day, and delayed them much. His face and hands were mortified from the cold, and he was utterly unable to proceed. They could not carry him, and he was evidently dying. He begged earnestly to be left behind; so they made a good fire, and gave him some of their food, as it was not at that time all consumed, and left him to his fate. Their provisions had been exhausted two days, when they saw an Indian's tent, and thought they should now get plenty. They came to it, and he offered them liberally all he had. His family consisted of himself, his wife, two children, and a dog; and his stock of food consisted of two partridges. His tent was near the bank of North or Nelson River, which they had to cross before they could reach York. This they expected to have found frozen, so that they could pass it at once; but the current being very rapid, there was no ice in the middle. Here then they had to remain until it was set fast quite across, which was not the case till a month after their arrival. They ate the two partridges, and when these were finished, there was nothing left. Sometimes a rabbit or two, sometimes a few lean partridges, were all the provisions for the day, for the whole party, and there were many days on which they caught nothing.

At length the dog was condemned, executed, and quartered; and the party being divided into four, each took a share. One of the messes consisted of the leader of the party, one of the ship's apprentices, who told me the story, and a man. Their leader had taken the fore quarter, which had one half the head and brain attached. As he went out of the tent, the curtain which served as a door, fell, and struck the dog's head, and the half brain fell upon the ground. The boy was quite alive to this, and thought "That's a windfall for me, if I say nothing about it." It was his business to fill the kettle with snow for cooking; and he took it up, remarking to the man who was in the tent, "I think I'll go and get some snow." When he came near the door of course his foot tripped, and he fell down, picked up the brain, and grumbling at his fall, went outside the tent where he could not be seen, and devoured it as it was, and thought it delicious. He never mentioned it till after their arrival at York, where they got plenty of food. He then told one of the party, through whom it was repeated to the leader, whose first salutation afterwards was, "Why, you rascal! you have been eating my brains." "Of course, sir, I did, I found them lying on the floor.

Would you not have done the same thing, if you had seen them in the same place?" The dog was finished all but one leg, before they reached York. Two men were sent forward to try and get some provisions, as the rest were too weak to travel fast; but they did not know how soon the supplies would arrive. A consultation was held as to whether this leg should be boiled that day, or kept till the next; but the first was decided upon from the advice of one of the party—"I think we had better boil it now, and trust to Providence." It was boiled, and the same day they received from York what they so much stood in need of.

Hospitality is a leading feature in an Indian's character. If he has food he shares it with any one who has none. If he has none, and sees another Indian who has any fish, for instance, he says, "I am going to take one of your fish;" and scarcely thinks that he is receiving a favour, or the other, that he is conferring one, in allowing it.

After being blocked up by the ice for seven weeks, and experiencing many heavy gales, it was at length so much broken up, that we were able to get through it, and we arrived at Moose, without any accident, on the 24th of September.

In the accompanying plate is shown our progress through the ice. The lines mark our course, and the figures are the dates on which we were able to know our position, by observations of the sun.

Moose is much prettier than York. It stands upon an island in the middle of the river, which is about three miles long, and from half a mile to

N 3

a mile broad. It is not built like York, in squares; though all the houses are made of wood. They lie upon the banks of the river, and extend nearly three quarters of a mile in length. Trees grow all around them, and there are little plots of

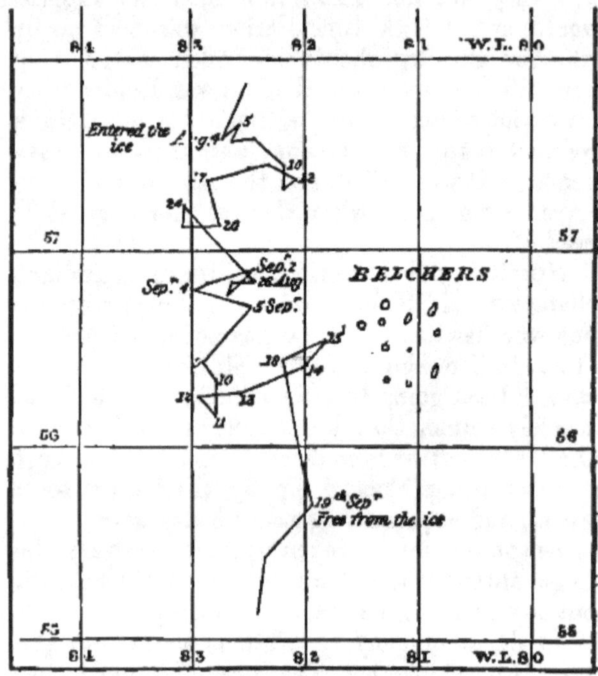

garden in front of many of the dwellings inhabited by the labourers. The ground is much drier and more fertile than that at York, and potatoes and turnips grow here without difficulty. Wild raspberries are very abundant in the woods, and the currant-trees in the garden are loaded with fruit.

The river is very shallow, and studded with many little islands, which are covered with wood, the openings between which are very pretty; and the variety in the tints of the leaves, which were changing rapidly when we arrived, added much to their beauty. The people here are more ingenious than at York, and make very pretty baskets of the bark of the birch-tree, which they ornament round the edges with quills dyed of various bright colours.

It is surprising for how many purposes the birch-bark serves. When stripped from the tree it is from a quarter to half an inch thick; but is capable of being split into a number of thin layers. The thick bark is used for making canoes; and the inner side, which is much smoother and finer than the outside, is employed for making these baskets, and round, flat, shallow trays, like decanter stands, which they call Rogins, and which answer many useful purposes, as cups, &c. If they hold the bark near the fire it becomes soft, and can be rolled up like cloth. They split it into thin layers, and sew these together, end to end, with roots or sinew, and then roll the whole length together. This serves as a tent. It occupies very little room, and lies easily in a canoe, when the Indian is travelling from one place to another. When he stops at night, he holds his roll near the fire, and as soon as it is warmed he can unroll it, and setting it upon its edge, he makes it into a round tent. By cutting it at first so that one edge is longer than the other, it has this shape, when set up, and he can light his fire in the middle, and lie under the sloping sides quite secure from the rain. The bark contains a good deal of turpentine, and is perfectly water-proof. There is another purpose to which they have lately begun to apply it. Many of them have been taught to write, and they use this as paper. They make a very thin layer of it, and having warmed it, rub it while still hot with any smooth substance, when it takes a high polish, and can be written upon.

The canoes are different in shape from those used by the Esquimaux. They are turned up at the ends, and are round-bottomed; and, instead of sitting down in them as an Equimaux does, the plan is to kneel upon the bottom. The cross pieces are merely to keep the sides apart. If anybody should sit down upon them, the canoe would immediately upset. They only draw two or three inches of water, and feel so unsteady, that one unaccustomed to them would be afraid to turn round to speak to anybody who is behind him in the same canoe, lest he should roll over. I found this out practically one morning. I intended going down the river to shoot some golden plover, of which there were many feeding upon the banks; and, having laid the gun in the bottom of the canoe, got into it, and knelt down near its head. A gentleman on the shore called out, "You had better take an Indian with you; you will not be able to manage alone." But, however, I "*had never dreamt*" of being upset in a canoe; so I thought I could manage very well. When I had approached the bank, and felt the bottom of the canoe touch the ground, I thought I might safely stand up to step out, and accordingly rose up. But my presumption was now punished; for as soon as I changed my position, it rolled over, and deposited me very quietly upon the bank, with no more serious inconvenience than that of getting wet through, and filling the gun with water; which was deep enough for both these purposes, though not sufficiently so to drown me. Fortunately the gentleman did not see my misfortune, and did not know of it until I mentioned it after dinner, when we could all laugh at it together.

We had very little expectation of being able to return home, as there was no probability that all the ice was dispersed which had detained us in the outward voyage; and we set off, after taking in our cargo, rather with the intention of doing our best, than with any prospect of succeeding in the attempt. Whilst we lay at Moose, there were, however, several high gales; and these, together with what we had experienced in the bay, had been sufficient, as it proved, to break the whole of it. We had strong winds all the way up the bay, and sailed in about twelve hours through that portion which had occupied us seven weeks in coming out. It was remarkable that we did not see the smallest particle of our old adversary, and we passed through Hudson's Strait without meeting any obstruction. On the 9th of November we landed in London in perfect safety, having had the most difficult passage to Moose which had been experienced for upwards of a hundred years, and having often proved the truth of the beautiful language of the Psalmist:

"He giveth snow like wool, and scattereth the hoarfrost like ashes:

"He casteth forth his ice like morsels, who is able to abide his frost?

"*He sendeth out his word and melteth them: he bloweth with his wind, and the waters flow.*

"Oh! that men would, therefore, praise the Lord for his goodness, and declare the wonders that he doeth for the children of men."

NOTES.

Note A.—P. 86.

The power of consuming so much animal food, and the necessity which exists for it in these cold countries, is not difficult of explanation. When a person breathes, a quantity of oxygen gas is absorbed from the air into the lungs, and an equal quantity of carbonic acid gas is expelled. The oxygen thus taken into the lungs combines with carbon contained in the blood, and forms the carbonic acid gas. But whenever oxygen and carbon unite, a good deal of heat is formed. Now this carbon in the blood must be constantly supplied, or the person would soon be starved to death. Flesh consists of carbon and water, and some other things which exist in very small quantities. The body is continually wearing away, and we require food to replace what is lost, and to support our strength. The particles thus removed are absorbed by the blood, which then contains carbon to combine with the oxygen taken into the lungs by breathing, and the combination causes heat. If a person takes severe exercise his body wears away faster; there is more carbon in the blood; he breathes more frequently, more heat is formed, and he becomes hot, as we say,—from taking exercise. But if he does not take food, he soon becomes thin, for his body is continually wearing away. Some of the carbon in the blood may, however, come from the food, if it contains much of it. Now bread, flour, vegetables, oil and tallow, or grease of any kind, contain a large quantity of carbon; whilst flesh contains comparatively little. If a person eats flesh and bread, or any kind of vegetable, the flesh goes to supply what has been worn away in his own body, and the bread, &c. supply carbon to the blood, for keeping up the heat. If, however, he cannot get any of these kinds of food which contain so much carbon, he must take so much exercise as to wear away his body, until a sufficient quantity of carbon is formed in the blood to answer this purpose; and he must take a very large quantity of flesh to replace what his own body has lost. We can now see the reason why, in these cold climates, people are so fond of oil and tallow, and why the Esquimaux will drink train oil, or eat whale's blubber, with so much pleasure. The grease consists principally of carbon, and thus supplies the blood with what is necessary for keeping up warmth, without the necessity for taking such violent exercise. The people say that two or three pounds of meat and one pound of bread would satisfy them as well as eight or ten pounds of meat without the bread. In the remote parts of Hudson's Bay, if a messenger is sent with letters from one fort to another, which occupies him perhaps a fortnight, he receives as a treat, when he arrives at the factory, a couple of pounds of flour, if there is any, and half a pound of grease or tallow, which he makes into some kind of pudding, and enjoys exceedingly. Truly the *necessaries* of life are not many!

It may appear to be wandering from the subject to speak of the fondness of people in hot countries for oil. The Italians, for instance, for olive oil; and the Caffres, in South Africa, for grease of any sort. This seems rather like a contradiction; but if we examine it carefully we shall see that it is not so. In hot climates exertion is very fatiguing, and the people cannot bear so much exercise as in a colder one: their bodies waste away less quickly, and less carbon is absorbed by the blood. What is necessary, therefore, for keeping up the proper degree of heat, must come from the food. We find, therefore, that such people do not eat so much flesh, for there is not much waste to repair; but they live principally upon vegetables, as fruits, and oil, which furnish the requisite quantity of carbon. If they did not take this kind of food, they must take more exercise to waste their bodies faster, and this would cause much discomfort.

Note B.—P. 102.

This may be thought, by some persons, to be quite incredible. There is, however, a substance well known to every medical man which has a somewhat similar power. Nitrate of silver, or common lunar caustic, may be swallowed in small doses for several weeks, without producing any apparent effect. After this time the skin becomes of a dull violet colour, which can never be removed. There are several persons now living who have become coloured in this way. The poison from the bite of a mad dog is said to be capable of remaining in the system for twelve months, without showing itself; at the end of which time the sufferer may become mad, and die of hydrophobia.

Note C.—P. 103.

It is possible for a person to sustain a much more severe injury than this whilst drunk, without being aware of it. I have seen a man's leg cut off, in consequence of an injury which occurred to him, whilst intoxicated. The next morning he was highly indignant with the nurse for trying to persuade him that it was not still there. After a day or two he acknowledged that she had spoken the truth, when he saw the stump, on the removal of the bedclothes for the purpose of dressing it.

APPENDIX.

[The following account of the means by which a ship's course is directed, and her position ascertained whilst at sea, has been placed in an Appendix, that it might not interfere with the general thread of the Narrative.]

As soon as the sea began to look green, we heard a fresh sound all day. It is only this colour in shallow water; and when this is the case, it is necessary "to keep the lead going," which means to see continually how deep the water is, that you may not strike upon the bottom. The way in which this is managed is easily understood. A man gets over the side of the ship, and stands in what are called "the channels," which means really "chain walls." These are broad, thick planks, which are fastened outside the ship, and through which the chains pass, by which the bottom of the rigging is fastened into the ship's sides. He then has a belt in front of his chest, the ends of which are made fast to the rigging, so that he may easily lean forward over the water without any danger of falling in. In his hand he takes a piece of lead, about eighteen inches long, and shaped like a very thin sugar-loaf, at the bottom of which is a hole, filled with tallow or dripping, and a long cord, or "lead line," is tied to the small end. He swings this lead backwards and forwards, until it has gained such force, that he can throw it a considerable distance from him into the water, towards the head of the ship, and as soon as he lets it go, he allows the line to be dragged into the water along with it, keeping hold of the end, that he may not lose it. The lead of course falls down to the bottom; and just when the ship in sailing past brings him up with it, he draws up the line till he feels it touching the bottom. Then he can see how deep it is, because there are little pieces of coloured cloth tied to the line at regular distances; and he counts these as he draws the lead up again. Whilst the lead rested upon the bottom the tallow became covered with whatever was there; so that when drawn up they can see whether there are shells, or sand, or mud, or hard clay, sticking to it; and if none of these are seen, they conclude that the bottom is rocky. The men have a peculiar sort of sing-song tone in which they call out how deep it is, that the captain or pilot may know. "By the deep, nine" means, that it is nine fathoms deep. A little further — "Quarter less nine;" and then, in a little time,—"By the deep, eight." Then, when it becomes very shallow, the song is changed, and they call the number of feet instead of fathoms, "Eighteen feet," and so on. It is very hard work throwing the heavy lead, so each man is only "in the chains" for half-an-hour or an hour at the most, and is then relieved by another man. If any part has been well sounded and marked down in a chart, the captain can tell exactly, or very nearly, where he is, even if it is quite dark, and he has not been able to take an observation for some time. For instance, in the British Channel;—suppose he did not know where he was, he would sound, and find, perhaps, that there were eighty fathoms, with a sandy bottom; he would go a little further, and find seventy-five fathoms, and sandy bottom; a little further, and find ninety fathoms, and brown muddy bottom. Then he would look in his chart, and see where eighty and seventy-five fathoms and sand were followed by ninety fathoms and mud; and when he found these, he would know exactly where he was.

There is something which seems very mysterious in the conducting a ship across a wide ocean, with so much certainty, when there is no land to steer by, nor anything which seems likely to help you. Perhaps this difficulty, like many others, may be found to be greater in appearance than reality. Two or three methods are adopted, which differ considerably from each other. The first is called "dead reckoning," and the others depend upon observations of the sun, moon, or stars. Of late years a still further improvement has been made by the invention of chronometers, or watches, which are so carefully made as not to lose or gain time irregularly. But whichever plan is used, we must first understand how to steer by the compass. When a bar or needle of steel has been rubbed with a loadstone, or a magnet, it becomes a magnet itself, and then, if placed in such a way that it can move, it turns one end towards the north. A thin bar of steel, therefore, is taken, which is five or six inches long, and an inch broad, and a small hole is made in the centre of its under side, so that it will balance when placed upon any small point (fig. 3.) Upon its upper side a round card is fastened, which is divided into four quarters, and N. or north, S. or south, E. and W., are printed upon these quarters. Each quarter is again divided into eight; and lines are drawn upon the card to each of these divisions, which are marked with letters thus: half-way between north and east is called north-east, and marked N.E.; half-way between north and north-east is called north north-east, and is marked NN.E., twice as much north as east; half-way between north-east and east is called east north-east, and is marked E.N.E.; and when it is between this and east, it is called east by north, or E. by N., to show that it is nearly east, but a little north at the same time. North by east, or N. by E., means nearly north, but a little east; and so it would be if we took it between north and west; only then we must say west each time instead of east.

The card is fastened to the bar, or needle as it is called, so that the N. shall lie upon that end which points towards the north. When this is done it is put into a round box, in the bottom of which is a pin, which goes into the hole on the under side of the needle. This box is about four inches deep, and a straight black line is painted down its inside, which is called "the lubber's line." This box is then fastened to the deck, in such a

o 3

position that the line points towards the head of the ship. A person looking at it sees nothing but the card, with these letters painted on it, for the needle is quite concealed; but as the card is fastened to it, it moves whenever the needle does, and we can always see by the N. on the card which is north, towards which the needle is pointing. Now as the needle always points towards the north, if we were to turn the box round it would still point in the same direction. If the ship were sailing north, the N. on the card would be close to the line in the inside of the box; but if we made the ship turn a quarter round and sail towards the west, the line would be moved to the W., and N. would appear to have gone a quarter from it. Now if we were to turn the ship another quarter, the line would be opposite S., and N. would be turned away from it as far as possible; and so on. But instead of turning it a quarter, we might turn it half a quarter, or less than this, and then N.W. or N.N.W. would be opposite the line.

Now let us suppose a captain wanted to sail from any place called A. to another place called B. (fig. 1.) He would wish to sail along the dotted line, which is the direct course. If we lay a ruler upon this line, we shall find that it will agree with W.N.W. or west north-west. He therefore tells the man who is steering to keep the ship in such a way, that the lubber's line shall be opposite to W.N.W. in the compass (fig. 2.) In the scale, in fig. 1, each mark means five miles. Let us suppose that he has sailed twenty-five miles in this direction; he will then have reached C. But now suppose the wind becomes so contrary, that the steersman cannot keep the ship's head in this way, and that instead of W.N.W. it is N.W. to which the line points. The captain asks him how he is steering, and he says north-west. He then takes his chart, and draws a line upon it, as we have done from A to C, and makes it twenty-five miles long. Then he puts his ruler along the line marked N. W, and rolls it up to C, and draws a line C D. Suppose he sails seventy miles in this direction, he will be at D. And now the wind becomes still more contrary, and the line is opposite N. He draws a line from D., in the same direction with N. on the compass, and finds that he sails, say thirty miles, in this direction. By this time he has arrived at E.; and now the wind changes altogether, and blows him towards the south, instead of the north. But still he wants to go west. Well, the steersman finds that the ship is sailing west south-west, that is, the line is opposite W.S.W., and they sail in this direction twenty miles, and he comes to F. Now he finds that he wants to go exactly west, and if the wind has become fair he is able to do so. The steersman turns the ship until the line is opposite W, and so he continues until he arrives at B.

But how is he to know what distance he has sailed? He finds this out by means of what is called the log (fig. 4,) which is a triangular piece of wood, having a piece of lead fastened to its lower corner, just heavy enough to make it sink, and then the wood stands upright when thrown into the water. Three strings are fastened to it, and are tied to a long string wound upon a reel. One man holds the reel lightly in his two hands, and the log is

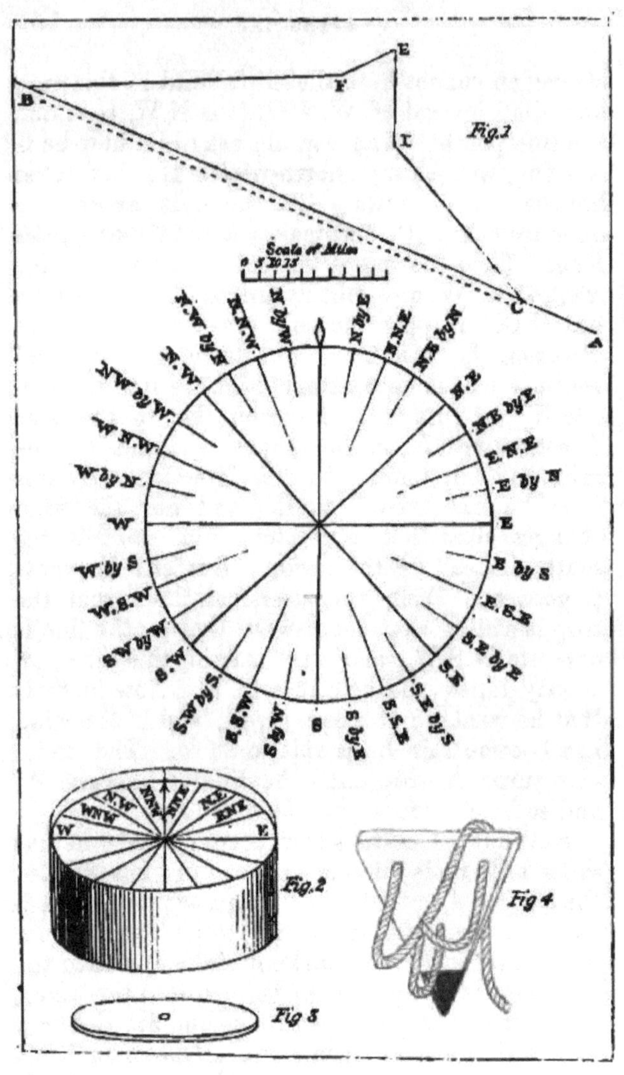

B
F
E
I
C
A
Fig.1
Scale of Miles
0 5 10 15
N by W
N.N.W.
N.W by N
N.W.
N.W by W.
W.N.W.
W by N
W
W by S
W.S.W
S.W by W
S.W.
S.W by S.
S.S.W.
S by W
S
S by E
S.S.E
S.E by S
S.E
S.E by E
E.S.E
E by S
E
E by N
E.N.E
N.E by E
N.E
N.E by N
N.N.E
N by E
W
WNW
N.W
NNW
NNE
N.E
ENE
E
Fig.2
Fig 3
Fig 4

thrown into the sea. The lead keeping it upright makes it remain where it falls, and the ship sails away from it, and as she sails away the string runs off the reel. Now this string is measured, and a knot is tied in it, at every forty-eight feet. In using the log then, a boy holds a sand-glass in his hand, which runs half a minute. As soon as the first knot touches the stern, the boy turns the glass, and as soon as all the sand has run through, the string is held tight, and no more allowed to run off the reel. The log is then dragged back to the ship, and the number of knots counted which have run out, and the ship is said to be sailing so many knots an hour. The reason is this: forty-eight feet is nearly the same proportion to half a minute that a mile is to an hour; so that if the glass ran an hour instead of half a minute, a mile of string would run off the reel, instead of a knot or forty-eight feet. If then five knots have run out, five miles would have run off; or nine knots, nine miles, and so on. Thus a knot is made to signify a mile. But if the sea is very rough, sometimes the string is jerked off too fast, or a wave carries the log back again towards the ship, so that it is not entirely correct. In this case there is another way of finding where she is, by observing the sun. The nearer we go towards the equator the higher the sun rises at noon; and the nearer we approach the poles, the lower it is at noon.

There is an instrument called a quadrant, which is so made that we can see the horizon and the sun at the same time, and find how high he is. And in this way the latitude or distance from the equator is found. It is much more difficult to find the longitude, or distance, east or west of any place. This is done by means of the chronometer. The world turns round once in twenty-four hours; and when it is noon with us, it is midnight with the people on the opposite side of the globe, as in New Zealand. Now, if it was noon with us, it would not be noon at a place to the west of us; for the sun would not be so high there as with us at that time,—it would still be morning there. But as the sun seems to come from the east, when it is morning with us, it is noon to the east of us; and when it is noon with us, the sun is leaving the eastern parts, and it is evening with them. The chronometer is set right at Greenwich before the ship sails; and as it goes with perfect regularity, it always shows what o'clock it is at Greenwich. We take an observation of the sun in the morning, and notice by our quadrant how high it is; and we see what time it is at Greenwich by the chronometer, when the observation is taken. We take another observation at noon, and find how high it is then. By this means we know how much it had to rise, when we took the first observation, and can calculate how long it would require *for it to rise* this distance. We can then tell what o'clock it was at the ship when we took the first observation; for, suppose we found it would require three hours to rise the distance between where it was then, and where it was at noon, we should know that it was nine o'clock at the time. Now, if the chronometer showed that it was nine at Greenwich, we should know that we were neither east nor west of it, but in the same longitude. If it was twelve o'clock at Greenwich, when it was nine with us, we should know that we were 2,700 miles west of it, or 45 degrees; for it is found by calculation that a difference of four minutes in the time, shows a difference of sixty miles in longitude; from which it is easy to calculate how many miles there would be, with a difference of three hours. It is possible to know where the ship is with great accuracy, by this means. When we were in Hudson's Strait, in going out, we telegraphed our consort to know what was her longitude. The answer was, "Seventy-five degrees and fifteen miles. What is yours?" Answer, "Seventy-five degrees and sixteen miles." On our way home, we met and telegraphed again, not having seen each other for nearly three months. "What is your longitude?" "Sixty-four degrees and twenty-four miles. What is yours?" "Sixty-four degrees and twenty-six miles."

The way in which questions are asked and answered at sea is interesting. Ships carry several flags, made of bunting, of different colours. One is blue, with a white square sewn in the middle; another white, with a blue square; a third, two white squares and two blue ones; a fourth, a blue, a yellow, and a red stripe; a fifth, all red; a sixth, yellow; and so on. There is a book which is carried by all ships that have colours, explaining what these mean. Thus, one flag means number one, another number two, and so on up to ten. Then in this book there are all kinds of questions and answers which are likely to be asked at sea, and a number is placed by the side of each. For instance:

1560. Are all well on board?
1561. All are well.
1374. What is your longitude?
1375. My longitude is ——.

Then the proper number shows the longitude; as 75, or 64, or whatever it may be.

1230. Can you spare us some water?
860. We have several men on board sick.
350. There is land ahead.

And so they go on. When a ship wants to ask, for example, the first question, the colour which represents 1 is tied to a rope, which passes through a pulley at the top of one of the masts; that representing 5 is tied below this; then 6; and then 0. When they are hoisted up, and the wind makes them fly out, the captain of the other ship sees through his telescope what flags are flying; and looks in his book to see what they mean. When he has found it out, he ties on his flags to answer; and in this way they can communicate, when they are one or two miles apart.

THE END.

R. CLAY, PRINTER, BREAD STREET HILL.

by Google

Google

Zeitfracht Medien GmbH
Ferdinand-Jühlke-Straße 7
99095 Erfurt, Deutschland
produktsicherheit@kolibri360.de